MEANING AND AUTHENTICITY

Bernard Lonergan and Charles Taylor
on the Drama of Authentic Human Existence

The language of self-fulfilment, self-realization, and self-actualization (in short, 'authenticity') has become common in contemporary culture. The desire to be authentic is implicitly a desire to shape one's self in accordance with an ideal, and the concern for what it means to be authentic is, in many ways, the modern form of the ancient question 'what is the life of excellence?' However, this notion of authenticity has its critics: Christopher Lasch, for instance, who equates it with a form of narcissism, and Theodor Adorno, who views it as a glorification of privatism.

Brian J. Braman argues, despite such criticisms, that it is possible to speak about human authenticity as something that addresses contemporary concerns as well as the ancient preoccupation with the nature of the good life. He refers to the work of Bernard Lonergan and Charles Taylor, thinkers who place a high value on the search for human authenticity. Lonergan discusses authenticity in terms of a three-fold conversion – intellectual, moral, and religious – while Taylor views authenticity as a rich, vibrant, and important addition to conversations about what it means to be human.

Meaning and Authenticity is an engaging dialogue between these two thinkers, both of whom maintain that there is a normative conception of authentic human life that overcomes moral relativism, narcissism, privatism, and the collapse of the public self.

(Lonergan Studies)

BRIAN J. BRAMAN is a professor in the Department of Philosophy at Boston College.

BRIAN J. BRAMAN

Meaning and Authenticity

Bernard Lonergan and Charles Taylor on the Drama of Authentic Human Existence

UNIVERSITY OF TORONTO PRESS
Toronto Buffalo London

© University of Toronto Press 2008
Toronto Buffalo London
www.utppublishing.com
Printed in the U.S.A.

Reprinted in paperback 2015

ISBN 978-0-8020-9802-3 (cloth)
ISBN 978-1-4875-2007-6 (paper)

Printed on acid-free, 100% post-consumer recycled paper

Lonergan Studies

Library and Archives Canada Cataloguing in Publication

Braman, Brian J.
    Meaning and authenticity : Bernard Lonergan and Charles Taylor on
the drama of authentic human existence / Brian J. Braman.

(Lonergan studies)
Includes bibliographical references and index.
ISBN 978-0-8020-9802-3 (bound). – ISBN 978-1-4875-2007-6 (paperback)

1. Authenticity (Philosophy).   2. Conduct of life.   3. Lonergan,
Bernard J.F. (Bernard Joseph Francis), 1904–1984.   4. Taylor, Charles,
1931–   5. Heidegger, Martin, 1889–1976.   I. Title.   II. Series.

B995.L654B73 2008   191   C2007-906271-7

University of Toronto Press acknowledges the financial assistance to
its publishing program of the Canada Council for the Arts and the
Ontario Arts Council, an agency of the Government of Ontario.

  Canada Council   Conseil des Arts
              for the Arts   du Canada

ONTARIO ARTS COUNCIL
CONSEIL DES ARTS DE L'ONTARIO
an Ontario government agency
un organisme du gouvernement de l'Ontario

University of Toronto Press acknowledges the financial support for
its publishing activities of the Government of Canada through the
Canada Book Fund.

Contents

Acknowledgments

For what is done through friends is our own doing.

– Aristotle, *Nichomachean Ethics*

The origin of this book dates back to my days in graduate school here at Boston College. As a graduate student I had the pleasure of teaching in our Great Books program. The first course in the four-year sequence is *Perspectives I: Perspectives on Western Culture.* The question that grounds this year-long course is the question that began philosophy: what is the life of excellence? After a couple of years teaching, I began to notice that the students reformulated this question about the best way to live in terms of self-realization, self-fulfilment, or being authentic. Once I finished my course work, I too began to think more about this ancient question in modern terms. Beginning with the writing of my dissertation and culminating with this book, this project has been a ten-year interrogation of this question: what is human authenticity? Admittedly, this book is a modest account, and in many ways just a beginning, of the nature of authentic human existence. Nonetheless, it is a beginning. And what has made this beginning possible is a number of men and women who – through their expertise, friendship, or both – have made this book a reality.

First, let me thank Ron Schoeffel, editor emeritus at the University of Toronto Press, for his patience and generosity of time and spirit in helping to bring this book to the light of day. I am grateful to all those readers whom Ron enlisted, for their insights, comments, and criticisms. They undoubtedly helped make this a better book. Under the category of expertise, I would like to thank Regina Knox for her editorial assistance. Her editing kept me on track.

viii Acknowledgments

Combining both expertise and more importantly friendship, I want to thank Joe Flanagan, S.J., Pat Byrne, Fred Lawrence, Kerry Cronin, and Thomas Hibbs not only for their unwavering support and encouragement but also for being living examples of what Lonergan thought authentic human existence ought to look like.

Finally, I wish to thank all my students who have passed through my classroom and my life. It was because of them and their own questioning and questing that brought forth in me my own set of questions concerning the best life and the desire to live it. While I have been abundantly blessed by all of my students, there are five who need to be thanked by name. It is in their friendship, their honesty, and their genuine concern for the good of the world that has kept me humble and prodded me ever to excel: Kathleen Yesinko, Mea Mustone, John Kleiderer, Michael Petit, and Grace Simmons.

In the end, however, there are two people in my life who have, more than any other person, showed me what human authenticity looks like: my wife, Peggy, and my father, Arthur James Braman. What these two have given me is beyond measure and impossible to repay. It is to both of them that I dedicate this book.

MEANING AND AUTHENTICITY

Introduction

Doug Rossinow, in his book *The Politics of Authenticity*, claims that the concept of alienation is key to understanding the rise of the new left after the Second World War, particularly in the 1960s. The alienation felt by the radical left of the 1960s was not the type of alienation associated with the economic or political alienation felt by the poor and by black Americans. The radicals of the sixties were largely an affluent group. Their experience of alienation 'was an estrangement less from dominant social norms, or from conventional political activity, than from their own real selves.'[1] For the new left, then, the overcoming of this sense of alienation meant the search for self-authenticity: what did it mean for them to be truly themselves, to be authentic?

From the beginnings of the new left to present-day culture, this desire to be authentically one's self has become commonplace. The concept of authenticity permeates the whole of culture.[2] Whether in advertising, political life, or the moral life, to be authentic is to be true to some higher standard; it is to be the genuine article. To speak about the desire to become an authentic human being suggests the need to overcome a dichotomy between what you are and what you want to be. It is to overcome both personal and cultural alienation.

This quest for authentic human existence does not, however, just spring up with the radical left of the 1960s. The idea of authenticity has a history. The idea of authenticity began to develop towards the end of the eighteenth century and was built on earlier forms of individualism, such as the individualism of Cartesian disengaged reason, or the unencumbered political individualism of John Locke, which sought to make the person's will prior to any and all social obligation. While authenticity has its roots in these sources, it is the child of the Romantic period. Romanticism, while still celebrating the individual, was extremely critical of those more exaggerated forms of individualism. As a correction, Romanticism sought to find a source deep within each of us that would connect us to something greater than ourselves. What comes out of the Romantic period is certainly a stronger sense of individualized identity, but an identity understood as neither punctual nor disengaged. Not only do I possess an identity that is peculiar to me, but also there is a unique way for me *to be*. Unlike the earlier forms of punctual individualism, however, Romanticism sought to index this unique way of being myself to something greater than one's self. In general the Romantic tradition sees 'human beings as set in a larger natural order ... with which they should be harmony.'[3]

It is with Jean-Jacques Rousseau and Johann Gottfried Herder that we see the idea of self-determining freedom, as tied to a unique way of being one's self, lay the groundwork for the later development of the idea of authenticity. For both thinkers, if I am not true to myself I somehow miss the point of my life. Being true to myself means that I must be true to what is original about me, as an expression of 'being' itself, and it is only I who can discover and articulate what is my original way of being in the world. 'What the voice of nature calls us to cannot be fully known outside and prior to our articulation/definition of it. If nature is an intrinsic source, then each of us has to follow what is within; and this maybe without precedent. We should not hope to find our models without.'[4]

However, it is the German philosopher Martin Heidegger who is most instrumental in making this question of human authenticity prominent within and without philosophical circles. Because Heidegger has been so influential, historically, in beginning the conversation about the nature and meaning of human authenticity, rather than give a short presentation here, in the first chapter I will offer a more lengthy account of his notion of authenticity, particularly in light of the later contributions of Charles Taylor and Bernard Lonergan to this ongoing conversation about what actually constitutes authentic human existence.

To repeat, the language of self-fulfilment, self-actualization, self-realization, and authenticity is now common linguistic currency in contemporary culture. However, this notion of authenticity is not without its critics. Christopher Lasch speaks of the 'cult of authenticity' as just another form of narcissism. Allan Bloom equates authenticity with self-centredness and the collapse of the public self. 'Robert Bellah and his co-authors probe this erosion of the political in their *Habits of the Heart*. The primacy of self-fulfillment, particularly in its therapeutic variants, generates the notion that the only association one can identify with are those formed voluntarily and which foster self-fulfillment.'[5] Daniel Bell sees authenticity as a 'megalomania of self-infinitization which consists in the refusal to accept limits, in the idea that nothing is forbidden and all is to be explored.'[6] Each individual is now considered the highest good, and the enhancement of this uniqueness has become the ultimate value. Moreover, the idea of authenticity is discounted by the post-structuralists, deconstructionists, and philosophical postmodernists – Foucault, Derrida, Lyotard, Rorty – because the term 'conveys the illusory myth of a totalizing, harmonious, unitary self, which they seek to replace with the image of a fragmented, plural, centerless and irreconcilably split subjectivity.'[7] It is with Theodor Adorno, however, where we find the most extensive and passionate criticism of the 'jargon of authenticity.' Let me explain.

For Adorno, this cult of authenticity is a magical and impoverished form of theological discourse. Merely by chanting the term, one is able to make present in its totality the hidden Absolute.[8] In other words, authenticity has become a sacred word with a sacred content; the sacredness of this content is manifested in the mere utterance of the term. 'Whoever is versed in the jargon does not have to say what he thinks, does not even have to think it properly.'[9] Truth and Transcendence are collapsed[10] into this one term. This idea of human authenticity is really a corrupted form of religiosity. As in a pseudo-religion, one needs only to profess belief; it makes little difference what one actually believes. It is sufficient for the act of believing to merely use the term; it is as if by merely uttering the word you are automatically what you speak.[11] What is profoundly absent, however, is the judgment as to whether what one claims to be is in fact the case. In the end, authenticity is merely a secular religion emptied of all transcendence. It 'preserves itself in an unreflected manner and elevates limitation, which abhors reflection, to the level of virtue.'[12] In short, the authentic ones suffer under the illusion of a mystical participation in the Absolute.

Besides this illusion of mystical participation in the *Mysterium Tremendum*, Adorno also sees an irony in those who are held under the sway of the jargon. Those who see themselves as authentic think the term is immune to the dehumanizing effects of mass communication, when in fact, more often than not, 'the authentic ones' find themselves, much as Rousseau understood, living out a type of 'consumerism that not only has a special claim on the spirit,' but is linked to what others esteem.[13] There is a further irony in the jargon. Where Heidegger saw authenticity as a bulwark against the 'they' and against small talk, he failed to foresee that what he named authentic would become[14] just another form of idle chatter. The jargon of authenticity protects the person from the 'disagreeable task of expressing himself seriously on the matter at hand, about which he knows nothing … The jargon which is not responsible to any reason, urges people higher simply through its simultaneously standardized tone.'[15] This jargon of authenticity supports and reassures a pernicious self-righteousness in which the person thinks he has achieved this all by himself as an unencumbered free person.[16] The jargon further inoculates the 'authentic one' from the self-realization that what he is doing is in fact 'bleating with the crowd.'[17]

Finally, this idea of authenticity is solipsistic. It glorifies the person who claims to be authentic. Not only is the glorified person the ground of being for the term, but she is 'the addressee of the term as well.'[18] In addition to this solipsism, the jargon is also a form of sophistry. Of course the 'authentic ones' profoundly repudiate any and all forms of sophistry, 'but they drag its (authenticity) arbitrariness along in their program: man is the measure of all things.'[19] Philosophically, then, the jargon claims there is an identity of truth and word, when in reality the jargon is only a cover story for arbitrariness.[20] Under the 'mask of the jargon any self-interested action can give itself the air of public interest of service to man.'[21] As a mask, the jargon actually covers over the 'suffering of the human condition by its own unreflected self-righteousness.'[22] So authenticity is identical with subjectivity per se. Subjectivity then becomes the judge of authenticity. This identity, however, between subject and object is circular. Since authenticity is denied any objective normativity separate from the subject, 'authenticity is determined by the arbitrariness of the subject, which is authentic to itself.'[23] 'Authenticity is a manner of behavior that is ascribed to the being-a-subject of the subject, not to the subject as a relational factor.'[24]

In spite of the ongoing criticism, however, the idea of human authenticity persists. Yet what is needed is not some uncritical acceptance, nor wholesale condemnation of the idea of authenticity, but a more adequate understanding of the real meaning to authentic human existence, one that takes seriously the intellectual, moral, and religious aspirations of the person. Still, why be concerned about the real meaning of authenticity? Given a culture of excessive 'affluence, mass consumption, the bureaucratization of many areas of social life, and increasing disengagement from political participation,'[25] a society's understanding of what it means to be authentically human will not only shape its institutions, but the solutions to its problems. The importance in clarifying what authenticity rightly means in terms of human living, then, lies in our common destiny as men and women. Understanding authenticity rightly has enormous consequences for issues of development and decline.

Why Charles Taylor and Bernard Lonergan? Taylor and Lonergan, like Gadamer and Heidegger, 'underscore the intimate link in philosophy, theology, and ordinary living between careful reading and the way human beings personally and communally ask practical questions about the right way to live.'[26] In other words, like Heidegger, Taylor and Lonergan are struggling to make sense of our lives by engaging in a 'primordial self-inter-pretation that settles the issue of "the one thing most needful" (Lk 10:42).'[27] Taylor and Lonergan take seriously the contributions of moder-nity, as well as the criticism of postmodernity.[28] But neither is content to accept certain postmodern claims 'that one must simply accept the irre-ducible plurality of cultures, values, and disciplines'[29] and eschew the ques-tion of a normative human existence: authenticity. In fact, Lonergan and Taylor think this desire to be authentically human does not by necessity lead to either narcissism or moral relativism. Both thinkers understand that our *Existenz* is a being-in-the-world of normative meanings and values. Where Taylor sees human authenticity grounded in a self-determining freedom that is ordered to something greater than the self, i.e., something noble, virtuous, or courageous,[30] Lonergan understands authentic human existence as authentic self-transcendence expressed in a three-fold form of conversion that is intellectual, moral, and religious. For both thinkers, however, authentic human existence is something deeply intimate, 'more intimate perhaps than one has explicitly conceived. Such existential speak-ing cannot be tidily tucked away into a category: at once it is psychological, sociological, historical, philosophic, theological, religious, ascetic, perhaps for some even mystical; but it is all of them because the person is all and involved in all.'[31]

To repeat, chapter 1 will give an overview of Heidegger's interrogation of the meaning of human authenticity. Chapter 2 will be a more detailed account of Taylor's genealogical rehabilitation of what is best and viable in modernity's approach to human authenticity. Chapter 3 will trace Loner-gan's transcendental understanding of what constitutes authentic human existence. However, both of these chapters, while important in their own right, merely set the conditions for the fourth chapter. Here we will place Taylor and Lonergan in conversation with each other in order to reinforce the important and perhaps surprising similarities, as well as crucial differ-ences that exist between these two thinkers. Placing them in conversation with each other can only help deepen, enrich, and push forward the ongo-ing conversation on what really is the life of excellence.

1

Martin Heidegger:
The One Thing Needful

Whether he likes it or not, and often, a singer must harbour
Cares like these in his soul; not, though, the wrong sort of cares.
— Friedrich Hölderlin, *Homecoming*

'Heidegger's tremendous impact on German philosophy in the early 1920s was inseparable from his concern with *conversio vitae* ... In his Gadamer biography Jean Grondin evokes Heidegger's farewell speech to his students upon departing from Freiburg for Marburg: "It began with the words: *To be awake to the fire in the night* ..." Heidegger spoke further of "fire and light, of brightness and darkness," and the mission of man to take a stand between the disclosure of Being and its withdrawal.'[1] For Heidegger, then, the importance of authenticity (the *conversio vitae*) resides in the need to provide a foundation for fundamental ontology – the question of Being. Moreover, the question of what it means to be authentic cannot be separated from the issue of Dasein, being-a-whole-self. This issue is further compounded by the fact that Dasein is not only a *questio mihi sum* (I am a question to myself), but is a burden to itself.[2] Moreover, the possibilities for an authentic life, *the truth of existence*, are located within the context of the Anyone, the 'they.' In other words, as a burden to itself and a question to itself, Dasein (there-being) can never fully grasp its possibilities outside the context of the 'they'; yet the 'they' is shot through with misinterpretations and misunderstandings. Finally, Heidegger offers us an account of what authentic historicity might be, in order to overcome this dialectical relationship of authenticity to inauthenticity, and bring to light the *truth of human existence*.

Dasein's Being-in-the-World

It was 'Nietzsche's pitiless and severe style of thinking which focused philosophy on the depth and fullness of life.'[3] The same may be said of Martin Heidegger after he emerged from his extensive meditation upon the thought of Nietzsche. In fact, the question of authentic human existence does not begin from some theoretical stance, the Cartesian project of self-doubt, for instance, or an ahistorical 'state of nature' narrative in the manner of Locke, Hobbes, and Rousseau. Rather the starting point ought to be this 'depth and fullness of life,' how the person is situated in the actual here and now. Heidegger's approach to the question of authentic (*Eigentlichkeit*) or inauthentic human living, then, begins by first describing the lived and concrete situation of the person. Heidegger calls this situated entity *Dasein* (there-being) because it alone has a unique comprehension of Being. 'Man is a being who is immersed among beings in such a way that the beings that he is not, as well as the being that he is himself, have already become constantly manifest to him ... manifest, that is, in their Being.'[4] Heidegger's phenomenological account of the person, Dasein, prescinds from metaphysical categories such as substance (*ousia*). Rather, Dasein is described as an event, a dynamic movement towards the possibility of being a Self that is whole.[5] 'Dasein is an entity which does not just occur among other entities. Rather it is ontically distinguished by the fact that, in its very Being that Being is an issue for it.'[6] To say that Dasein's being is an issue for it is to say that Dasein must confront the fact that what it is to be is an open question – a question that needs to be settled ultimately by Dasein itself – a question of self-interpretation.[7]

For Heidegger, Dasein does not appear upon the scene fully constituted in its being like the Cartesian or Lockean subject that seems to manifest itself *ex nihilo*. Rather, Heidegger begins his interrogation of the being of Dasein by situating Dasein within a historically and culturally languaged context that is already given. This is Dasein's being-in-the-world, and it is this primordial and lived context in which the question of authenticity is to be ultimately raised. It cannot be adequately addressed outside of this lived matrix.

Heidegger begins his interrogation of this lived matrix (*Lebenswelt*) with a phenomenological account of Dasein's being-in-the-world as *Everydayness* (*Alltäglichkeit*) or *Averageness*. Everydayness is understood as the day-to-day activities of Dasein within an already constituted set of relations. This daily set of relations that constitute Dasein's mode of Everydayness is more than a duality of either familial or occupational relations. Everydayness is a much richer relational context that 'indicates the manner in which There-being is initially disclosed to itself by reason of its coexistence with others, in the comings and goings, the constant superficial exchanges which constitute daily intercourse ... It is consummate ordinariness.'[8] This 'consummate ordinariness' in all its myriad expressions is Dasein's day-to-day and moment-to-moment mode of being human.

Heidegger is quite clear that in spite of the fact that Dasein's being-in-the-world is relational, these relations are often opaque and unthematized. More importantly, they can be covered over and distorted by the lived mode of Dasein's Everydayness. Heidegger sees this distortion occurring in such notions as 'idle talk and curiosity.' 'Heidegger asserts that the true function of language is to let beings "be appropriated in a primordial manner." When not devoted to this task, language degenerates into gossip, rumor and empty reflection.'[9] In other words, language should let beings manifest themselves in a most basic and primary way and thus enable Dasein to appropriate its world for itself. On the other hand, 'idle talk and curiosity' suggest that Dasein uses language to dissipate itself, so to speak, in the mundane aspects of human living with little or no reflection. 'We often at first listen tolerantly to someone's idle talk, so as not to give offense to the weak; but then we gradually become attracted [advertimus]. The smallest thing may divert [advertit] me from some serious thought.'[10] Dasein seeks to hide from itself and avoid the burden of its own being by immersing itself in an unreflective preoccupation within the humdrum aspects of day-to-day human living. Again, such activities as idle talk and curiosity are ways in which Dasein keeps itself inoculated against the fact that it has surrendered itself to what Heidegger has termed das Man (they-self) of human existence.[11]

While Everydayness is the lived context of Dasein's being-in-the-world, ironically it also refers to the natural tendency of Dasein to conceal 'things, to regard them superficially often accepting what everyone says about them.'[12] This propensity of Dasein to dissipate itself in the crowd is expressed through Heidegger's notion of das Man. Heidegger's term das Man explains the fact that Dasein at any moment of its existence finds itself already in an a priori context of meaning that has been predetermined and pre-interpreted. The 'They' (das Man) has already decided the manner in which Dasein should live out its existence. The They, while seemingly an amorphous and ambiguous term, is in the concrete something that determines and settles questions concerning what things are valuable, what roles are worthwhile, and what projects are important to pursue. What is pernicious about this situation is that the They hides the manner in which it has tacitly relieved Dasein of the burden of explicitly[13] choosing what it wishes to be as a being. 'The They renders everything common, comparable, interchangeable.'[14] A levelling effect takes place; all that is unique and creative is stifled. A certain drive towards homogeneity takes place, which in turn encourages mediocrity and complacency. Because of Dasein's already constituted immersion in this they-self, Dasein automatically and unreflectively surrenders its own potentiality for being a true Self in order to 'dwell in tranquillized familiarity.'[15] In short, the they-self relieves Dasein of the burden of its own Being.

Heidegger uses the categories of *Everydayness* and *das Man* to describe Dasein's predicament with respect to its being-in-the-world. Yet the real question concerning what type of being or self Dasein is to have, is predicated upon something prior to the aforementioned analysis of Everydayness. The answer to the question about the meaning of the being of Dasein is conditioned upon first asking what it means for Dasein to have a *world.*

Dasein is a being 'whose nature is to-be-in-the-World.'[16] *World* for Heidegger is the total set of relations, or field, in which human living takes place.[17] 'When we say that There-Being is "in" the world, "in" here has by no means a purely spatial sense ... but rather the sense of to be "at home" or to sojourn in, to be entrusted with a privileged familiarity with the World-about.'[18] Only through having a world, which is an organized whole, a context of meaning, is it possible for Dasein to have a relationship to its own being, and the being of others. World is something that belongs essentially to the structure of Dasein. Just as Dasein is not the solitary Cartesian ego, neither is it some Leibnizian monad without any nexus of relations. 'It is a profound intimacy of There-being with the World, by reason of which other beings that are within the World may be "encountered" [that is] reveal themselves for what they are when they come in contact with There-being.'[19] In other words, Dasein's first concern is with things of the world, 'only through the world can it relate to, or assume an attitude toward its own being ... it [the world, which is a matrix of meaningfulness] is essentially Dasein-orientated.'[20] It is only as being-in-the-world that Dasein is able to discover beings, and thereby discover itself as a being within the horizon of Being.[21] The world is 'a non-ontic, non-thematic, pre-disclosed *there*, where Dasein encounters those things with which it is preoccupied, and which are meaningful as well as purposeful for Dasein's own coming and goings, its basic intercourse with the world-about.'[22] The impossibility of constructing an identity is central to Heidegger's critique against any form of self-constituting Cartesian ego that is punctual and self-illuminating. Heidegger's critique of the Cartesian form of identity 'reveals that there can be no immediate self-knowledge arrived at through introspection or reflection. Our direct understanding of ourselves is always the product of a template of traditional schematizations which circulate as common sense in our culture, and tend to distort and disguise as much as they reveal.'[23] In other words, the traditional concept of a subject as developed by Descartes and Kant posits the self as an ego that is the identity and stability of a being that is always a mere entity and non-relational. For Heidegger, 'Dasein's ego is the entire phenomenon, existentiell and existential.'[24] Whatever one's identity, it is an identity that is structured by and remains within the confines of the Anyone. Dasein is never a subject in terms of substance; Dasein is a configuration of interpretations, the source of which is *das Man*. The Anyone offers what it considers valuable, worthwhile; it provides a set of norms and practices that shape Dasein's being-in-the-world. However, Dasein's desire to-be-a-whole-self cannot be fully understood outside a deeper and more primordial exigency of Dasein as being-toward-the-end. Dasein is *Sein-zum-Tode*.

Unlike Descartes, who sought the foundation and continuity of his own identity within the *cogito*, Dasein's own identity, its-being-a-self, is grounded in the world. Only by having a World can Dasein have a Self; the Self and World are coterminous and together they constitute a matrix of meaningful relations 'within which There-Being comprehends both itself and other beings, that There-being enjoys a radical familiarity.'[25] In short, Dasein needs a World in order to know who it is, let alone what it is.[26]

Part of having a World for Dasein is also to have a project. Being-in-the-world means that Dasein constitutes itself in the making and doing of everyday living, which is manifested in and through various projects. A project for Dasein is the 'something-to-be-brought-about, something-to-be-accomplished.' More often than not, these projects are not something that Dasein explicitly averts to in its day-to-day interchange with the world. Generally, Dasein takes little notice, either cognitively or affectively, of its surrounding environment. Yet this environment 'consists in a manifold of reference which determines what can be done; in proceeding to work Dasein submits to these references without explicitly recognizing them.'[27] The World, then, is organized around some fundamental human project that Dasein is meant to further; in addition, Dasein depends upon this project for its own being and the grounding of its identity.[28] Projects are the vehicles that carry Dasein 'away from the present into an indeterminate and illusive future.'[29] By having a project, Dasein is always ahead of itself; it is always seeking to bring to fruition some future goal or idea; as a result, Dasein's immediate relationship to human living is one of distraction and preoccupation.[30]

The various projects that Dasein has within its World suggest that Dasein is essentially caught up in day-to-day 'practical activities' that are oriented towards the future. 'Practical activity is the immediate way in which Dasein exists and the original way it encounters things.'[31] Another way of understanding the issue of practical activity is to see it as a 'vision of prudence.'[32]

In this vision, beings manifest themselves as instrumental.[33] These beings form a complex set of relations understood as purposefulness in relation to any of Dasein's projects. 'For Heidegger, we do not live in a world of objects; we live for the most part, in a ready-to-hand context of equipmental relations organized into a web of means/ends relations.'[34] Prudential vision is the way in which Dasein understands how the various means/ends relations fit into an intelligible whole, how they work to bring about various projects. Human existence, then, is to be seen in all its complexities as 'essentially teleological; in each of our actions we express goals which point outward to some sense of our lives as a final, definitive configuration of meaning.'[35]

It is clear that the structure of Dasein's being-in-the-world is an already constituted set of meanings and values that orbit around issues of human purposefulness. It is a world already structured around a prior set of having-been-made-decisions. 'Dasein confronts a world which is already determined in its essential structure and must decide within the concrete range of possibility which such a world affords.'[36] Dasein's projects, and the practical activities necessary to bring these projects about, are already circumscribed for Dasein when it comes upon the scene. Dasein thus finds itself in a 'limit-situation.' The choices/decisions it must make about its various projects, among which is the project of its own being, are already delineated by an a priori temporal givenness. Yet to say that Dasein has this type of structure still does not address the question of Dasein's own being. There is still need to articulate what is essential to the being of Dasein, particularly with respect to its being-in-the-world.

The Structure of Care

According to Heidegger the very structure of Dasein's being is one of care (*Sorge*). 'Dasein's Being is care.'[37] For Heidegger this structure of Dasein's being as care is irrefragable. To say that Dasein is care means that the world in which Dasein finds itself is ordered around what Dasein considers to be most pressing in terms of its 'there-being.' 'This concern for being – in the first instance its own – sets Dasein apart from every other being, which simply is what it is with out being concerned for what it is or is to become. It is only by virtue of this essential concern ... that Dasein can relate to other beings or even to itself.'[38] Dasein is not to be thought of as primarily a particular being, but more as a possibility of being such and such, which offers its Self to itself for realization: 'Dasein can become itself only by realizing that its being is uniquely and properly its own. All this is implied in the notion of concern, which is the essence of being there.'[39] Put another way, 'man's Being is not from the beginning a *fait accompli* but something that he himself must achieve, a task in which he can default.'[40] Dasein as care reveals to Dasein its potentiality-for-being-a-whole-self. It also reveals that the essence of Dasein is relational; it is a way of being, rather than a mere 'what' of being.[41] Dasein is in the world only through being with it in care. Care is 'both a relation "to being" and an obligation to be.'[42] Again, this possibility-for-being-a-whole-self, and the fact that Dasein's Being is an issue for it, is structured by *Sorge*. *Sorge* points to Dasein's awareness of its responsibility for its own-most possibilities. *Sorge* reveals that not only is Dasein responsible for its own Being, but also it is the source of its own possibilities. What does it mean, then, to say that Dasein is the source of its own possibilities? It means Dasein is burdened with the responsibility for its being such and such. Yet this responsibility for being-a-whole-self is paradoxical. The paradox resides in the context of Dasein as being-in-the-world. Dasein is responsible for its own possibilities-for-being-such-and-such, but these possibilities reside outside of Dasein.

> In language ... there is hidden a way in which the understanding of Dasein has been interpreted ... Proximally, and with certain limits Dasein is constantly delivered over to this interpretedness, which controls and distributes the possibilities of average understanding and the situatedness belonging to it ... This everyday way in which things have been interpreted is one into which Dasein has grown in the first instance, with never a possibility of extrication. In it, out of it, and against it, all genuine understanding, interpreting and com-municating, all re-discovering and appropriating anew, are per-formed.[43]

It is not enough, however, to say that the being of Dasein is care. For care itself has a structure. Care comprises Dasein's sense of being thrown (its facticity), Dasein's sense of existence (*Existenz*), and Dasein's awareness of its fallenness.

'Dasein's Being is care ... As being, Dasein is something that has been thrown; it has been brought into its "there," but not of its own accord.'[44] It is *thrownness* (*Geworfenheit*) that captures Dasein's already-constituted lived situation, which is not of its own choosing. Every interpretation Dasein has of itself is already mediated by a 'forestructure' of anticipation and presup-positions about what issues might be at stake.[45] Dasein's thrownness is the forestructure through which is mediated Dasein's interpretation of itself and its World. Dasein has been thrown *into existence*. It exists as an entity that has to be as it is and as it can be. But this burden that Dasein carries with respect to being as it can be is not something borne in isolation. Dasein can be itself only in the context of its thrownness. This condition of thrownness is something that Dasein can never transcend. All of its choices and decisions will continually be made within this horizon. Dasein in this state of thrownness is brought face to face with itself 'as a potentiality-for-Being as the entity which it is.'[46] To reiterate, Dasein in its day-to-day living, its facticity, finds itself saddled with the burden of having to make choices. Dasein must choose 'to be' from a range of already constituted possibilities. While it is true that Dasein's being is not a fait accompli because Dasein ultimately bears the burden for its own becoming, nonetheless, it is not correct to assume that Dasein then constitutes itself and its world in its entirety. Thrownness means that Dasein already finds itself to a large degree constituted by a pre-understood set of meanings and values that structure the World as given.

Just as thrownness is constitutive of care, so also is Dasein's existence as *Existenz*, which expresses Dasein's peculiar relationship to things. Dasein is not merely present alongside other things within the World, but it is also present to things by virtue of its standing out from them and relating itself essentially to them.[47] *Existenz*, then, is a term Heidegger uses to show that Dasein is a being that exists outside of itself, beyond itself. It projects itself. In all distinctive human activities, those myriad ways of self-realization, whether loving, knowing, planning, or worrying, 'Dasein is always outside itself, beyond itself, in advance of itself as a being.'[48] A proper understanding of *Existenz* means more than the mere 'is-ness' of Dasein. *Existenz* properly formulated refers to Dasein's potentiality-for-being. The *Existenz* for Dasein suggests that Dasein is a being that is 'already-ahead-of-itself.' Just as Dasein's world is organized around some fundamental human project, so also is Dasein projecting itself towards the realization of its Self as a whole.[49] The implication here is that Dasein is free to choose to be either a whole self – that it is a self that has appropriated and accepted the conditions of its own being – or an inauthentic self, which would be Dasein's complete self-surrendering and immersion in *das Man*: a concealment of its self from itself.[50]

If *Existenz* is as Heidegger indicates a potentiality-for-being-a-whole-self, this suggests that Dasein is responsible for making this potentiality actual. This leads Heidegger to speak of this potentiality-for-being-a-whole-self as 'mineness.' 'Wherever there is human being – wherever being is *there* – there is a unique focal point of events and situations, a unique possibility of realization, and this is conveyed in the expression *mine*.'[51] Mineness points to the primordial situation where Dasein is not only essentially referred to beings, but it is also 'referentially dependent upon them.'[52] 'Mineness' further reinforces the basic fact that Dasein is responsible for its own most being. Choices and decisions are made in the context of being mine; I am responsible for what it is I am to be. Yet paradoxically, this notion of mineness and its concomitant sense of responsibility seems to be undermined by the last element to the structure of care: *fallenness* (*Verfallenheit*).

Fallenness, unlike thrownness, which is the givenness of Dasein's being-in-the-world, shows Dasein to have surrendered itself to the Everydayness of human living. Dasein has fallen into, been absorbed by, the *They*. Again, such notions as 'idle talk, curiosity and ambiguity characterize the way in which, in an everyday manner, Dasein is its "there" – the disclosedness of Being-in-the-world ... In these, and in the way they are interconnected in their Being, there is revealed a basic kind of Being which belongs to Every-dayness; we call this the *falling* of Dasein.'[53] The category of fallenness points to an unreflective set of choices/decisions whereby Dasein has moved away from its potentiality-for-being-a-self to fall into, as it were, the humdrum flow of day-to-day occurrences that are the hallmark of Every-dayness. 'Fallenness into the "world" means an absorption in Being-with-one-another, in so far as the latter is guided by idle talk, curiosity, and ambiguity.'[54] Thus, while mineness points to Dasein's responsibility for its own most being, the notion of fallenness suggests that Dasein conceals from itself this responsibility and exigency for being a whole Self.

In analysing the structure of care (*Sorge*), something about Dasein's being-in-the-world has been revealed. Yet these are not the only categories that help us to uncover what it means for Dasein to be in the world. There is one more important category to be discussed with respect to how Dasein's situation in the world is opened up – the question of *Stimmung* (mood).[55] According to Heidegger, mood not only binds Dasein to the world, but it reveals the facticity of Dasein's existence. Again, facticity refers to Dasein's existence as it is confronted with the demand for deci-sions in the face of a World not of its own choosing, but still it must choose; Dasein is delivered over to the fact that it has to be.[56] 'Dasein finds itself (*sich befinden*) in a certain situation which represents the concrete range of its possibilities. This situation (*Befindlichkeit*) is the chrysalis of Dasein's being and it is reflected in the mood.'[57] Dasein is a being that is always and wholly immersed in mood. 'Mood itself is a constant reflection of *being there*.'[58] Mood opens Dasein up not only to the world but also to itself. 'It is the basis of man's affective life, rendering him susceptible to the encoun-ter of things, allowing him to be touched, moved.'[59] Another way to under-stand what mood might be is through the phrase 'ontological dis-position.'[60] Through Dasein's ontological disposition, the world of beings keeps obtruding upon human living. This disposition makes manifest 'how one is, and how one is faring.' 'In this "how one is," having a mood brings Being to its There.'[61]

Through Dasein's various moods the 'There' of its being is consistently revealed to itself, whether thematized or not: mood orients Dasein to its world. 'Ontologically mood is a primordial kind of Being for Dasein, in which Dasein is disclosed to itself prior to call, cognition, and volition, and "beyond" their range of disclosure.'[62] For example, the feeling of dread (anxiety) can reveal to Dasein its own stark contingency. Anxiety usually manifests itself through Dasein's experience of some form of dissolution. Dissolution means that the familiarity, the stability of Dasein's world of meaning, is ruptured and the facticity, the overpowering contingency of Dasein's existence, is revealed. Dissolution is the experience that one's very own being is dissolving or slipping away. Through the ontological disposition of anxiety, Dasein is confronted by the possibility of its own nothingness, its own arbitrariness, and its own radical finitude. In other words, its fallenness, its facticity, and its thrownness are revealed in and through anxiety. Because Dasein's being is normally characterized by distraction and its preoccupation with Everydayness, it is only through some type of rupture, reflected in a particular mood, that the *There* of Dasein is revealed and only then will Dasein be able to move to a position of openness vis-à-vis Being, and beings.

While anxiety reveals that one element of Dasein's being is the threefold structure of care, there is another mood that reveals something even more primordial concerning the being of Dasein: the fundamental mood of guilt. To Heidegger, guilt is at the core of Dasein's Being. This mood announces that Dasein is a being that lacks wholeness, completeness. Guilt is rooted in the 'not' that Dasein is: not-being-what-one-should-be.[63] More will be said about guilt when the discussion turns to the issue of authenticity itself. For now, suffice it to say that mood in general 'reveals the nothingness which lies at the heart of our own being, the burden of Being.'[64]

If, as Heidegger maintains, Dasein's lived Self is more often than not in terms of the 'they-self,' then for Heidegger most human beings are living an inauthentic mode of existence. To surrender one's self over to the *They* is to opt for a 'less-than-mode-of-being-in-the world.' Conversely, Heidegger's notion of human *authenticity* (*Eigentlichkeit*) pivots upon Dasein's awareness of its own 'potentiality-for-being-its-self.' The first movement towards an authentic mode of human living involves Dasein coming to understand that it is responsible for its own being. Dasein must realize that it is 'its own possibility,' and this is something it can 'choose or lose itself.'[65] The question of authenticity discloses, as it were, to Dasein the fact that what it is to be as a human being resides within Dasein itself. Dasein is burdened with deciding and choosing what it means for it to be a particular type of entity. This authentic 'being-one's-self' 'takes the definite form of an *existentiell* modification of the *they*.'[66] Dasein begins to take possession of its own most possibility of being other than what it is. However, this is not to suggest that Dasein is omniscient. On the contrary, the question of

Dasein's authenticity is always bound to its experience of *Geworfenheit* and the givenness of its world. Dasein's own potentiality for being a Self may be chosen or may be surrendered, but the struggle for authenticity is always circumscribed by Dasein's finitude, its thrownness, and its World. Paradoxically, there can be no absolute escape from the they-self to discover one's own possibilities, precisely because the They is the source of all possibilities, whether authentic or inauthentic.[67] According to Charles Guignon in 'Heidegger's "Authenticity" Revisited' it is 'clear that what Heidegger is attacking is not the role of the Anyone in constituting concrete possibility,' but the way in which we unreflectively appropriate the culturally constituted sets of meanings and values and thereby close off our own responsibility for our lives.[68] The transcendence of Dasein is thus to be understood in the context of its finitude.

This question about Dasein's authenticity concerns not only Dasein's potentiality-for-being-such-and-such, but also Dasein's own understanding in terms of the for-the-sake-of-which it chooses. Three elements constitute this for-the-sake-of-which. Firstly, there is what Heidegger calls the prior disclosedness. It is what is already disclosed as a possibility for Dasein's choosing. In other words, this prior disclosedness is a broadly constituted a priori horizon of possible choices for Dasein to make. Secondly, this disclosedness reveals something specific that Dasein can actually concern itself with, and that this something lies within the domain of Dasein's possibilities. Lastly, Dasein projects its possibility for being such and such towards the 'entity willed.'[69] Again, whether Dasein chooses to be authentic or not is a decision always made within the context of the world, and Dasein's world is shaped by its for-the-sake-of-which. This is to say that the possibility of Dasein's being-its-self 'pertains to the ways of its solicitude for others and of its concern with the *world*.'[70]

Rupture and Authenticity

It is one thing to say that authentic human living begins with the awareness of one's own 'potentiality-for-being' and quite another to show how one might arrive at this juncture. Because Dasein's normal mode of human intercourse is mired in the they-self, something is needed to jolt Dasein out of its lethargy, out of its enslavement to a they-self. 'The Self emerges only with the breakdown of the self.'[71] This breakdown takes place in an experience of dissolution, which occurs most palpably in an encounter with death. One must bear in mind that the experience of dissolution through death is not necessarily relegated to the actual physical event, even though the awareness of one's own earthly demise is also crucial to Dasein's transformation to self-possession. Death is that moment when Dasein confronts the contingency of human reality in all of its complexity. It is an 'experience of nothingness.' Heidegger uses the example of a broken instrument to show how Dasein can be brought out of its unreflective mode of being-in-the-world. As long as the instrument functions as it should, one never has to confront the fragility of the world of meaning that binds it. But should the instrument fail, Dasein's project and its world are ruptured; Dasein then experiences a sense of displacement or lostness, because the broken instrument has revealed the tenuousness of its own being-in-the-world. While this example may sound somewhat puerile, it helps to show that when meaning of any kind is ruptured or destroyed on any level, what is revealed is the precariousness of Dasein's own World, the *dark night* of human living. Projects and other expressions of meaning are revealed to be rootless. At a more profound level, the loss of a set of meanings or values, which bind Dasein to a World and give Dasein a Self, exposes it to an ever-deeper realization of the fictive nature of its own existence. This type of death experience ought to enable Dasein to face the arbitrariness of its own existence, as well as facing the burden of having to chose its own potentiality-for-being.

Concomitant to the death of meaning is also the awareness of the inevitability of one's own physical death; this in turn reveals the fragility of all of Dasein's choices and projects. In short, Heidegger considers death to be the primordial horizon out of which human authenticity is made possible.[72] Death forces Dasein to face its own potentiality-for-being. There is nothing guaranteed concerning Dasein's fate. Dasein exists continuously under the possibility of not-being. Given the constant threat of passing into nothingness, Dasein may either choose to take hold of itself and make decisions concerning what it wishes to be in light of its own contingency, or continue to surrender itself to the 'ubiquitous They.' Heidegger sees Dasein as 'being-towards-death' (*Sein-zum-Tode*), which is at the same time being-towards-a-possibility of being-a-self.[73] To face death squarely, Dasein becomes resolute in the face of its own tenuous existence. Resoluteness 'brings us before the primordial truth of existence,'[74] which is that one must choose always in the light of death: a choice that could be finalized at any moment because of one's demise. Death frees one from entertaining the nonessential, the incidentals of life. Ironically, one's future is opened up 'towards-oneself existing as the possibility of nullity.'[75] Dasein chooses its own possibilities for being such and such in the light of its own potential nothingness.

The rupture in one's world, either through the encounter with physical death or the loss of meaning, opens Dasein up to the possibility of being authentic. However, this rupture also opens Dasein up to something more primordial, more basic, and that is the call of conscience. Conscience is that voice of Dasein that reveals to it its responsibility for its potentiality-for-being-a-self, and thus Dasein's way to authentic existence. The voice of conscience is likened to 'Dasein's everyday interpretation of itself.'[76] Another way of understanding the notion of conscience is as a call. The call of conscience has the 'character of an appeal to Dasein by calling it to its own most potentiality-for-Being-its-Self.'[77] As call, conscience discloses to Dasein its they-self and the subsequent need to break away from this mode of being-in-the-world, this inauthentic form of existence. This is to say, Dasein now confronts itself as the being that must decide what it wishes to be, how it wants to constitute its own most Self. Authenticity (*Eigentlichkeit*) in the context of this call means that the Being of Dasein is determined 'by the way it relates itself to the task of living by taking a concrete stand on its life as a whole.'[78]

> Through disclosedness [of conscience], that entity which we call *Dasein* is in the possibility of *being* its *there*. With its world, it is there for itself, and indeed – proximally and for the most part – in such a way that it has disclosed to itself its potentiality-for-Being in terms of the 'world' of its concern.[79]

The call of conscience is to Dasein's own self. This call, according to Heidegger, is something that comes from me, yet it is beyond me and over me in the context of the world. The call of conscience is an unthematized dynamic that pulls Dasein back to itself, to gather its self to itself. It summons Dasein to realize its own possibilities. It must not be assumed, however, that the call of conscience has a specific content. The call itself is indefinite, it is a call to possibilities, but it does have a sure direction – it is directed to Dasein itself. This directedness 'to the Self in the They-Self does not force it inwards upon itself, so that it can close itself off from the external world. The call passes over everything like this and disperses it so as to appeal solely to that Self which ... is in no other way than Being-in-the-world.'[80] Again, it must not be assumed that the call of conscience is anything like a communication. Unlike communication, which has something to say, a content, the call of conscience is without content. It 'asserts nothing, gives no information about world events, has nothing to tell.'[81] The call of conscience is to be understood more in terms of discerning the various pulls and counter-pulls that are exerted upon Dasein, particularly with respect to its choices concerning authentic or inauthentic existence.

> Yet what the call discloses is unequivocal, even though it may undergo a different interpretation in the individual Dasein in accordance with its own possibilities of understanding ... When 'delusions'

> arise in the conscience, they do so not because the call has commit-
> ted some oversight (has mis-called), but only because the call gets
> heard in such a way that instead of becoming authentically under-
> stood, it gets drawn by they-self into a soliloquy in which causes get
> pleaded, and it becomes perverted in its tendency to disclose.[82]

Finally, the efficacy of this call of conscience seems to be predicated upon
a certain type of resoluteness in the face of what the call reveals. 'By "resoluteness" we mean letting oneself be called forth to one's ownmost being-
guilty. Being-guilty belongs to the being of Dasein itself, and we have determined that this is primarily a potentiality-for-Being.'[83] Thus to be resolute
means that Dasein allows itself to encounter itself as ontologically guilty.
This guilt can be either authentic or inauthentic. Being-guilty is analogous
to the Greek notion of *hamartia* (missing the mark). Because Dasein always
lags behind its own most possibility-for-being-a-self, it is always less than
what it should be. Guilt is the experience either explicitly or implicitly that
Dasein is always off the mark with respect to what it wishes to be. Guilt is
constitutive of Dasein's being because Dasein is always and everywhere
guilty of not being what it should be. Thus one is authentically guilty if the
call of conscience has been heeded and Dasein chooses to bear the burden
of its own possibilities, which also means the appropriation of one's own
death. But because the authenticity of Dasein is to be determined with
respect to the whole of *Existenz*, then even there Dasein is still guilty; it
always falls short in the light of that whole.

> There-being comes to its achievement in authenticity, insofar as it
> permits a strange uneasiness that steals upon it from time to time to
> estrange it from the ontic distractions that fill its every day, chooses to
> hearken to a voice that comes from within itself to tell it that it can
> transcend these beings unto Being but can never transcend its fini-
> tude.[84]

On the other hand, inauthentic guilt is characterized by the surrendering
of one's own potentiality-for-being-a-self in favour of the they-self. Here
Dasein is culpably guilty because its choice, even though unthematized, is
to surrender the possibility of being-a-whole-self in favour of fallenness.
  Authentic existence for Heidegger means that Dasein is not merely
present to the things that are constitutive of its world. Dasein is present to
things by virtue of standing out from them and relating itself essentially to
them; Dasein is present to the things of its world by being authentically
present to itself through Care. The possibility of an authentic existence
comes about through recognizing the ways in which Dasein surrenders the

burden of being a Self over to the they-self. This self-revelation comes about most profoundly through Dasein's coming to understand its self as being-towards-death (*Sein-zum-Tode*).

Authenticity is never completely achieved. Heidegger's analysis of Guilt shows us that Dasein is a being that is always more-or-less an expression of itself. The irony here, however, is that 'since our way of interpreting ourselves and our world is mediated by social and historical categories and conceptualizations, our normal self-evident self-interpretation is more often than not a misinterpretation.'[85] Thus, authenticity and inauthenticity always belong together; they cannot be conceived in isolation from each other. Both are essential for the truth of Being to be made manifest, revealed. Dasein, then, is situated in a dialectical tension between these two modes of being-in-the-world. Thus inauthentic existence is itself revelatory and in that sense true. Not true in terms of the manifestation of truth as an event of Being. Rather, it is true because it renders 'things banal' and creates the background out of which the 'terrible and marvelous can burst forth.'[86] If Dasein's unappropriated world of meaningfulness is thereby ruptured, this leads to the possibility of an authentic existence for Dasein. What transpires in this moment is a clearing away of 'concealments and obscurities in order to become fully transparent about the *Truth of existence*.'[87] The *Truth of existence* for Dasein is the coming to light of the being that Dasein is in relation to Being in general. It is a performative form of truth, not propositional.[88]

As has been stated previously, because of the they-self, the meanings and values that constitute the givenness of Dasein's being-in-the-world have become reified, hardened by tradition. It is here that Heidegger makes the distinction between tradition and heritage. Authentic existence demands of Dasein a retrieval of its heritage over and against tradition. Tradition for Heidegger is what masks and covers and even encrusts those 'primordial well-springs' of Being.[89] Heritage, on the other hand, symbolizes those authentic possibilities that enable Dasein to be an authentic Self. To be authentic, Dasein 'must recover the deeper undercurrents of historical meanings that course beneath the fads and fancies of the *today* and take them over as the fundamental resources for its own being.'[90] Thus what is called for is an authentic sense of historicity.

Historicity and Dasein

Historicity means that Dasein is ultimately a temporal being. Who and what it is unfolds in the context of temporality. Dasein has a history. Authentic historicity implies that Dasein has to some degree turned around in order to face itself as a self that 'is-as-having-been.'[91] The retrieval that takes place within the context of an authentic understanding of historicity means that Dasein exposes the sources of its ways of being and then clarifies its possibilities for living a continuous, integrated, and unified Self. Authentic existence has a determinate content. This content is not to be understood as something ready-to-hand. Rather, the content is brought to light through Dasein's penetrating the traditional 'interpretations of its current World in order to retrieve the enduring ideals and aims of its *heritage*.'[92] Let us recall the basic condition of Dasein's being-in-the-world. 'Dasein must permit things to provide the binding direction of its conduct because its very being is such as to depend upon other beings, because it is essentially oriented toward the realization of itself outside or beyond itself in the midst of things it encounters within an arch of openness which it itself constitutes.'[93] This is Dasein's situation. Thus, the possibility of authenticity resides in Dasein's retrieval of a heritage as opposed to the tradition of the Anyone. As William Richardson points out, 'Historical there-being cannot achieve its own individual authenticity from the community. The heritage which there-being assumes in authenticity, then, is not simply its individual history but somehow the heritage of the entire people with which it is.'[94] Authentic Dasein understands its own Being as an expression of those historical possibilities within its heritage. It must not be assumed that heritage is a call for some set of old-fashioned ideas or values, or simply a retreat to the past. 'Heritage is the soil of an individual and of his community. The deeper people sink their roots into their heritage, the greater will be their own development' and understanding as human beings.[95] It is an appropriation of a heritage that provides Dasein with its possibilities for being-a-whole-self. Even though authentic Dasein remains contextualized in the given modes of understanding mediated by the Anyone, authenticity helps Dasein to see how the possibilities handed down to it by the Anyone are manifest only in a 'corrupt and distorted form.'[96] In short, the 'more authentically there-being in resolve consents to be what it is in all its finitude, the more profoundly this heritage becomes its own in a freely chosen discovery of the potentiality of its existence that is always immediately ending.'[97]

It is clear that only in the retrieval of a heritage is it possible for Dasein to be authentic. In *Being and Time* Heidegger states, 'The possibility that historiology in general can either be "used" for one's life or abused in it, is grounded on the fact that one's life is historical in the roots of its Being, and that therefore, as factically existing, one has in each case made one's decision for authentic or inauthentic historicality.'[98] It is possible, therefore, to understand Heidegger's notion of heritage in the light of Nietzsche's short essay 'On the Advantage and Disadvantage of History for Life.'[99] In other words, Heidegger, like Nietzsche, seems to reject normative and intelligible ends to the Being of Dasein, yet oddly enough he affirms these possibilities and 'cannot do without them; this pervasive tension both binds his thought together and tears it apart.'[100] Heidegger's notion of a heritage, then, is an attempt to provide an intelligible foundation for the being of Dasein.

Heidegger, like Nietzsche, assumes that the past is intelligible, that it makes sense. If not, why would Heidegger bother to distinguish between tradition and heritage? Thus history 'can serve life by providing a vantage point for identifying the characteristic weaknesses of one's own age and models for overcoming one's own time.'[101] Heidegger does not explicitly claim that historical knowledge must be understood in terms of morality or how one should live one's life, or even if morality has a knowable shape. In fact the 'whole task of *Being and Time* is to probe the ultimate ground of that unity (time) in order to gain access to the larger question – the first and, ultimately, only question that really interested him – the question of the ontological difference.'[102] Yet it seems to me, even within this context, that Heidegger thought that history should promote a higher form of life than mere life. The task then for the authentic human being is to recognize 'what his existence is – an imperfect tense that can never become a perfect one'[103] and to overcome this knowledge through authentic historicity. Another way to understand Dasein's retrieval of a heritage is under Aristotle's notion of *phronesis*. 'The task of *phronesis* now would be to discern deceptive concealment within revealment and deal with it as best errant Dasein could.'[104] In other words, authentic Dasein must fashion itself in the light of a true understanding of what it is for Dasein to-be-a-whole-self, out of the 'raw materials drawn from history in order to educate toward human excellence.'[105] This compact symbol of a heritage is Heidegger's attempt to answer the question, how is Dasein to comport itself authentically?

Lastly, the question of Dasein's authenticity also lies in its own awareness that its destiny is bound up with things in a way that cannot ultimately be controlled. When Dasein comes upon the scene it finds itself situated in an already constituted set of meanings and values not of its own choosing. As a result, it is in this context of being thrown that Dasein is to live out its destiny. In order for Dasein to live authentically, then, it must appropriate what is given 'to provide the binding direction of its conduct because its very being is such as to depend upon other beings.'[106] In short, Dasein's deepest possibilities of being-a-self in the proper sense of the term are always drawn from a shared repository of historical meanings, values, and possibilities that are mediated by and through culture. Dasein's 'personal quest for meaning [and authenticity] is in the final analysis only possible against the background of the communal projection of meaning of a historical people.'[107]

2

Charles Taylor: Ethics and the Expressivist Turn

Each mortal thing does one thing and the same:
Selves – goes itself; *myself* it speaks and spells,
Crying *What I do is me: for that I came.*

– Gerard Manley Hopkins

'What we possess, if this view is true, are the fragments of a conceptual scheme, parts which now lack those contexts from which their significance derived. We possess indeed simulacra of morality; we continue to use many of the key expressions. But we have – very largely, if not entirely – lost our comprehension, both theoretical and practical, of morality.'[1] This quote from Alasdair MacIntyre's *After Virtue* suggests that we live under the false assumption that we hold in common shared understandings of our moral terms and relations, and when we engage in moral discourse we are all operating from the same understanding of our common moral sources. But in fact we no longer share the same understanding concerning our moral meanings and values. We have lost, as he says, our comprehension because we no longer know the history of our moral sources.

While sympathetic to MacIntyre's argument, Charles Taylor seeks to push the conversation in another direction: Taylor's hermeneutical project is to uncover the sources of our moral identity, 'the sources of the self.' Taylor's concern is to uncover why we see ourselves and the world in which we live as we do; this means primarily raising the issue of the genealogy of our moral sources that shape our identities in a particular way: 'Selfhood and the good, or in another way selfhood and morality, turn out to be inextricably intertwined themes.'[2]

In Taylor's retrieval of the sources of our modern moral selves he is clear that modernity per se is not the problem, but the ways in which certain significant achievements have been distorted. For instance, the affirmation of ordinary life that came out of the dissolution of the medieval synthesis with its concomitant modern conception of freedom (which Taylor wants to endorse) has been transformed so that the person is to be understood as a disengaged subject, possessed of instrumental reason, who seeks self-fulfilment as an absolute right. 'The reason this vision is deeply confused is because it reads the affirmation of life and freedom as involving a repudiation of qualitative distinctions, a rejection of constitutive goods as such.'[3] Taylor's overall hermeneutical project is a thicker retrieval of a non-anthropocentric perspective, which, as he believes, 'philosophy since the enlightenment has been motivated to occlude.'[4] Taylor wants to move beyond a subjectivist form of morality in both its modernist and postmodernist versions, where all moral values are considered goods only if they are grounded in human powers or human fulfilments,[5] to a more 'authentic' understanding of the moral subject and his or her desire for self-realization. It is essential to recover the deeper moral vision of modernity: 'The genuine moral sources involved in the aspiration to disengaged reason or expressive fulfillment tend to be overlooked, and the less impressive motives – pride, self-satisfaction, liberation from demanding standards – brought to the fore. Modernity is often read through its least impressive, most trivializing offshoots.'[6]

Taylor finds in a genealogical and dialectical[7] account of human authenticity a significant way of extricating our moral self-understanding from the moral malaise that MacIntyre so clearly articulated in his *After Virtue*.

Retrieval of a Notion

We have seen for Heidegger that human authenticity is grounded in Dasein as *Sein zum Tode*. In order for Dasein to be authentic, it must appropriate to itself two fundamental elements. First, Dasein is a being that is 'embedded in a culture, a form of life, a "world of involvement," which means that Dasein ultimately must see itself as a being that is embodied.'[8] Second, one's finality is in terms of death and disintegration, and this structures the horizon for Dasein's acts of self-constitution and *phronesis*. Charles Taylor acknowledges his debt to Heidegger's insights into 'engaged human agency' and his importance in helping us 'emerge painfully and with difficulty, from the grip of modern rationalism.'[9] However, because Heidegger's position on human authenticity ultimately closes off the possibility of real transcendence, Taylor's interrogation of what constitutes authentic human living moves in a slightly different direction.

Taylor thinks the normativity of authentic human existence involves more than appropriating the finitude of one's own being. Contrary to the relativism that seems inherent in the idea of authenticity, there is in fact a moral ideal – a normativity – behind the desire for self-realization. What is needed is a recovery of the original ideal that lies behind human authenticity. Taylor wishes to uncover this original intention through an act of retrieval that is somewhat analogous to what Martin Heidegger means by a heritage. Heidegger distinguishes between a tradition – in which the meanings and values that constitute the givenness of Dasein's being-in-the-world have become reified, hardened, or even distorted – and a 'heritage.' The truth of human existence demands of Dasein a retrieval of its heritage that symbolizes those authentic possibilities that enable Dasein to be an authentic self. Dasein 'must recover the deeper undercurrents of historical meanings that course beneath the faces and fancies of the "today" and take them ever as the fundamental resources for its own being.'[10] For Taylor, the Heideggerian notion of heritage entails first uncovering the genealogy of our modern identity before one can properly settle the issue of what it means to be an authentic person. Because the modern understanding of authenticity is bound up so intimately with modernity's notion of identity and selfhood, the richness and complexity of the idea of authenticity cannot be grasped, 'unless we see how the modern understanding of the self developed out of earlier pictures of human identity.'[11] In *Sources of the Self*, Taylor traces the development of our modern understanding of the self with a remarkable depth and richness of scholarship. Taylor's historical account of our modern identity brings to the fore the historical roots of contemporary culture's preoccupation with self-fulfilment, self-realization – in short, with being authentic. In this acknowledged project, Taylor, like Heidegger, has indeed taken Nietzsche to heart: 'History belongs to the preserving and revering soul – to him who with loyalty and love looks back on his origins.'[12] Taylor, with this 'loving reverence' for our origins, finds that in spite of the seeming narcissism and excessive self-centredness that is often associated with authenticity, a proper understanding of this term does not by necessity lead to an aberrant form of egoism. Authenticity properly understood can shed a new and more ample light upon the project of human living. And the dangers that some critics[13] see in the rhetoric of authenticity are grotesque expressions of something positive and essentially human.

In order to show that the desire to be authentic is rich and fully human, Taylor begins by tracing the development of our modern identity.[14] In the course of this project, Taylor explains how the breakdown of the medieval synthesis and the rise of the modern subject provided the impetus for the birth of the notion of authenticity. Taylor sees the idea of authenticity arising at the end of the eighteenth century and 'it builds on earlier forms of individualism.'[15]

However, it was not until the rise of Romanticism that flesh and bone were provided for what later became the explicit language of authenticity. According to Taylor, what develops out of the Romantic period is a strong sense of individualized identity. This suggests not only that each of us possesses a peculiar identity, but also that there is the ideal of being 'true to myself and my own particular way of being,'[16] and that we are responsible for our own way of being. Taylor finds in Jean-Jacques Rousseau an early exemplar of this desire to be 'true to myself.' Rousseau speaks of human beings as endowed with a certain *sentiment de l'existence*, a direct moral feeling of right and wrong. For Rousseau, our 'moral salvation comes from recovering authentic moral contact with ourselves.'[17] More importantly, however, what comes out of this need to recover one's 'authentic' moral self is the idea of self-determining freedom. It is no longer enough to be merely in contact with one's *sentiment de l'existence*; one must now face the truth of one's own freedom. In other words, I am confronted by the fact that it is I who must decide what will shape me; and conversely, I must not surrender my freedom to external influences.[18]

If Rousseau laid the groundwork for the idea of authenticity, Johann Gottfried Herder takes the idea of self-determining freedom and concretizes it into the position that each of us has a unique and unrepeatable way of being a human being. 'Being true to myself means being true to my own originality. In articulating it, I am also defining myself, realizing my potentiality that is properly my own.'[19] Being true to one's self is almost an imperative. If, as Herder suggests, each of us has an original way of being human, then we are not only called but also somehow commanded to live our life not in imitation of anyone else. The imperative to be true to one's self underscores the point that if 'I am not [true to myself], I miss the point of my life, I miss what being human is for me.'[20] Moreover, not 'only should I not fit my life to the demands of external conformity; I can't even find the model to live by outside myself. I can find it only within.'[21] In short,

> being true to myself means being true to my own originality, and that is something only I can articulate and discover. In articulating it, I am also defining myself. I am realizing a potentiality that is properly my own. This is the background understanding to the modern Ideal of authenticity, and to the goals of self-fulfillment or self-realization in which it is usually couched.[22]

From this all too brief historical account of the development of the modern idea of authenticity, it should be clear that for Taylor the idea of authenticity is a rich, vibrant, and vitally important addition to any conversation concerning what it means to be fully human. Even in the face of examples in which this idea of authenticity seems to be a manifestation of Nietzsche's *last man*, what is needed is not a wholesale condemnation of authenticity, but a rediscovery of the truthfulness of this ideal, and its concomitant implications for substantive human living. Unfortunately, the current debate that swirls around this ideal fails to see beyond its cultural caricature. On the one hand, some view authenticity as nothing more than a cover story for self-centredness and moral relativism;[23] on the other hand, some champion the quest for authentic human existence by maintaining that individual choices concerning what one's authentic life is to be are not to be challenged. For the 'boosters,'[24] then, even to suggest that there might be something normative to what it means to be an authentic human being is to invite the possibility of repression. Yet Taylor is convinced that both positions miss the point with respect to authenticity. 'So what we need is neither root-and-branch condemnation nor uncritical praise; and not a carefully balanced trade-off. What we need is a work of retrieval, through which this ideal can help us restore our practice.'[25]

With Taylor's encounter with the diverse traditions, or sources, of our moral identities, he seeks to recover a notion of authenticity removed from the morass of self-centredness, moral relativism, and the assumed prohibition against asking the question about what is the best way to live that has now become the standard cover story to the meaning of human authenticity. Taylor locates his efforts above an apparent irresolvable contradiction, by offering his own picture of what 'authenticity' might be. Authenticity is 'a picture of what a better or higher mode of life would be, where better and higher are defined not in terms of what we happen to desire or need, but offer a standard of what we ought to desire.'[26] Taylor's view of authenticity expresses the conviction that terms such as *self-fulfilment* and *self-realization* are not just cover stories for narcissism, nor are they terms that justify a stance that is labelled the 'liberalism of neutrality.'[27] Authenticity is a moral ideal that ultimately answers the question of what constitutes the good life. In short, as with Heidegger, Taylor understands that acquiring a proper understanding of authenticity is getting at the truth of human existence.

The Structure of Identity

If, however, the ideal of authenticity is to be lifted out of its contemporary distortions, one must ask the further relevant question, what are the conditions in human life that facilitate the realization of an ideal of this kind? This question is at its root a question about what it means to have an identity. How do I see myself? What animates and moves me? What do I hold dear, and how am I defined by these various answers? To claim an identity is to proffer an understanding of who I am, and what my fundamental defining characteristics of being human are.[28] My identity is the ground that makes all of my tastes, desires, hopes, and opinions intelligible.[29] Yet to speak of having an identity in this way, am I not reinforcing the criticism that authenticity automatically slides into a pernicious form of individualism? Not necessarily. If, as Taylor states, having an identity entails an orientation to something other than myself, to properly define who and what I am, then discovering my own identity is not worked out in isolation. 'My own identity crucially depends on my dialogical relations with others.'[30] It is in this dialogical relationship that I come to know what matters to me, what is of utmost importance. 'If some of the things I value most are accessible to me only in relation to the person I love, then she becomes internal to my identity.'[31]

The question of identity may be looked at in two ways. First, the modern understanding of personal identity sees the *individual* as a natural being characterized by a set of 'inner drives or goals or desires and aspirations. Knowing what I am really about is getting clear about these. If I inquire after my identity, ask seriously who I am, it is here that I have to look for an answer. The horizon of identity is an inner horizon.'[32] The second approach is what Taylor calls the pre-modern. It regards persons as parts in a larger order. Without this order I would be less than human. Being situated within this defined order answers for me the deepest questions concerning who I am and what role I play in the drama of human existence. This horizon is external to me.[33]

For Taylor, the pre-modern understanding of identity is no longer tenable, but neither is the modern understanding. The subjectivism of modernity is a dead end. In order to overcome the modern and the pre-modern approaches to identity, Taylor offers an alternative: 'To define my identity is to define what I must be in contact with in order to function fully as a human agent, and specifically to be able to judge and discriminate and recognize what is really of worth or importance, both in general and for me.'[34] Identity, then, refers to certain evaluations that are the indispensable horizon or foundation for personal reflection and evaluation. Modernity's vision of the disengaged self – grounded on the model of self-clarity and control – contradicts that concrete being who grows and becomes. 'I can only know myself through the history of my maturations and regressions, overcomings and defeats.'[35] My identity is defined by those things that deeply matter to me. They provide the framework or horizon out of which I can judge what is good and valuable, and more importantly, they reveal how am I situated vis-à-vis what really matters to me – Heidegger's *Sorge*. However, the full definition of someone's identity involves not only 'his stand on moral and spiritual matters but also some reference to a defining community.'[36] The very possibility of my stand on what I consider to be an authentic identity is already constituted in 'a social understanding of great temporal depth ... in a tradition.'[37]

In taking his cue from Heidegger, Taylor points out that the person is not only languaged but embodied as well. Existence is a context of bodily and worldly relations. The condition of our being-in-the-world is that we 'be already engaged in coping with our world, dealing with the things in it, at grips with them.'[38] This is Taylor's own hermeneutics of facticity. In other words, society is the locus of an individual's identity, which means that our sense of self is grounded in a horizon or framework of meaning. A horizon is foundational because it is that 'in virtue of which we make sense of our lives spiritually. Without a framework, one falls into a life that is spiritually senseless.'[39] To operate within the context of a framework is to function with the belief that what we are doing or feeling is 'incomparably higher than the others which are more readily available to us.'[40] In short, our horizon is the background out of which we make choices about our identity, not the least of which includes moral judgments. While this is true, it should be pointed out that we are assuming a more differentiated account of the notion of horizon, as opposed to the unreflective appropriation of our horizon associated with Heidegger's *das Man*. The anonymous *they* 'maintains itself factically in the averageness of that which belongs to it ... because it is insensitive to every difference of level and of genuineness and thus never gets to the "heart of the matter."'[41] A horizon, then, expresses the particular ideal that is behind our intentions, choices, and reactions;[42] it shapes our sense of who we are and the moral realm we inhabit. It constitutes our normative idea of human authenticity.

There is another way of understanding the framework or horizon, and that is to see it as a set of answers to a set of questions that each of us may have regarding what is most important and worthwhile. For Taylor, each of us exists within a space of questions. Our various frameworks or horizons are the answers to these questions. Horizons are the background that give meaning and structure to our life, as well as articulate for us what we consider of worth, and how we are to understand ourselves vis-à-vis this background. To be truly a self, to be truly authentic, one needs to exist in a 'space defined by distinctions of worth.'[43] What it means for me to be authentic is 'defined by the commitments and identifications which provide the frame or horizon within which I can try to determine from case to case what is good, valuable, ought to be done.'[44] We define ourselves, then, by how we evaluate the aforementioned criteria. Recognizing the fact that we can make evaluations of this kind militates against the slide to moral relativism. Evaluations of the type that Taylor is suggesting indicate that we possess a sense 'that one way of acting or living is higher than others, or in other cases that a certain way of living is debased ... Some ways of living and acting have a special status, they stand out above others; while, in certain cases, others are seen as despicable.'[45] To have an identity, to be authentic means that we must choose and decide within a constellation of evaluations that are shaped by what we consider most worthwhile, important, good, truthful – our horizon. In fine, our identity is intimately connected to our ideal of authenticity, and authenticity refers to 'certain evaluations that are essential because they are the indispensable horizon or foundation out of which we reflect and evaluate as persons.'[46] Moreover, even 'the sense that the significance of my life comes from its being chosen ... depends on the understanding that *independent of my will* there is something noble, courageous, and hence significant in giving shape to my own life.'[47]

Our identity, and thus the issue of authenticity, is shaped by the decisions that we make about what is worthwhile; furthermore, these decisions arise within an already constituted foreground of self-understanding and self-interpretation. However, it would be wrong to think this process of self-constitution is as solitary as it might first appear. From Taylor's point of view, the ideal that structures a given orientation does not exist in a vacuum. The question of my being an authentic person does not reside outside the context of human relationships, and more specifically outside the community. As mentioned earlier, human existence is 'dialogical.' 'We become full human agents, capable of understanding ourselves, and hence of defining an identity through our acquisition of rich human languages of expression.'[48] Our community is constitutive of our identity. Our self-understanding is mediated by our ongoing interactions in community. We are languaged beings; the self can never be properly understood outside the context of a dialogical relationship.[49] Taylor notes, 'Community is constitutive of the individual, in the sense that the self- interpretations which define him are drawn from the interchange which the community carries on.'[50] In other words, 'each young person may take up a stance which is authentically his or her own, but the very possibility of this is enframed in a social understanding of great temporal depth, in fact, in a tradition.'[51]

To call ourselves dialogical is to assert Heidegger's claim that we are languaged beings. We are beings 'that somehow possess, or are the locus of, this constitutive power of expression.'[52] For Taylor, language is not to be thought of in terms of the classical designative view, represented by Locke, Hobbes, and Condorcet, in which 'language is an assemblage of separable words, instruments of thought that lie, as it were, transparently to hand and can be used to marshal ideas.'[53] Rather, language is to be understood according to Heidegger's notion of *Lichtung* (clearing). Language opens up spaces to set the conditions for something worthwhile, meaningful, to be disclosed about ourselves and the world we inhabit. Language gives access to meanings. It discloses: 'Language is seen as the condition of the human world being disclosed.'[54] This disclosure takes place between human beings; a world for us is disclosed. Language so understood is not to be misconstrued as another variant of Heidegger's notion of idle chatter, which is an implicit account of language as merely instrumental. 'Underlying both emotions and elations is another crucial feature of the linguistic dimension: it makes possible value in the strong sense ... only language beings can identify things as 'worthy' of desire or aversion. For such identifications raise issues of intrinsic rightness.'[55] By *intrinsic rightness* Taylor means 'we are able to "get things right" in language, by articulating a feeling properly, by evoking the right mood, or by establishing an appropriate interpersonal relation – many of which are not at all a matter of designating things.'[56] The rightness of language is foundational and primordial. It is the means by which a world is disclosed and constituted as a 'human world.'[57] It is the means by which the truth of human existence is revealed. Finally, Taylor understands authenticity as based on an ideal that structures my life in such a way that my choices and decisions are ordered around this ideal, 'so that I do what I ought to do, and not merely what I want to do.' But this raises the question of the truth of my choices. 'Taylor believes that there are truths-of-the-matter regarding the objective reality independent of human subjects, and thinks we can account for independent objects as they really are on their own. It is possible for human subjects to account for such objects independently of our interpretation of them because it is possible for us to transcend our subjectivity authentically, thereby incarnating objectivity.'[58] Truth is an act of disclosure. It is Heidegger's notion of the truth as *aletheia*. What is being truthfully revealed through a 'perspicuous articulation' is a framed representation, the truthfulness of which is predicated upon an accurate correspondence to reality.[59] In other words, to say something is true allows the object to be understood in its disclosedness: 'It is truth as contextualized disclosure.'[60]

The development of the modern identity has moved away from the older notions of an unchangeable framework 'where people saw this framework as enjoying the same ontological solidity as the very structure of the universe. But the very fact that what was once so solid has in may cases melted into air shows that we are dealing not with something grounded in the nature of being, but rather with changeable human interpretations.'[61] Because we no longer can speak of a 'normative nature'[62] under the old dispensation, Taylor has moved to a hermeneutical approach to show that to be an authentic subject is to be someone who not only makes distinctions of worth between higher and lower, but also someone who lives within an independent web of meaning and values that orient and ground self-understanding. In short, Taylor, along with Lonergan, agrees with 'Ortega y Gasset that culture sets problems which each generation must resolve either authentically or otherwise.'[63]

In sum, notions like the rugged individualist, or the 'punctual self,'[64] are atavistic; one's identity is always constructed linguistically, socially, and historically. The full measure and definition of someone's identity usually incorporate not only the stand one takes on various moral and spiritual matters, but it also includes some reference to a defining linguistic community.[65]

Moral Ontology and the Good

Up to this point, the reader may have received the impression that the choice of our identity and the horizon that structures it are both activities of clear self-understanding. This is not the case. Taylor is very much aware of the problem of self-deception. Self-interpretation is never some pellucid enterprise; it is an ongoing struggle of trying to understand which is a more 'illusion-free interpretation' of one's self.[66] This ongoing struggle for an 'illusion-free interpretation' is in fact an inherent tension within the ideal of authenticity itself. This 'tension comes from the sense of an ideal that is not being fully met in reality ... The fact that there is tension and struggle means that it can go either way. On one side are all the factors, social and internal, that drag the culture of authenticity down to its most self-centered forms; on the other are the inherent thrust and requirements of this ideal.'[67] Yet it is one thing to speak of this ideal as a source of tension, and quite another to ask where the ideal is to be found, so that one does not fall into the trap of soft relativism. Soft relativism is the view that everybody 'has his or her own values, and about these it is impossible to argue.'[68] This position goes hand in hand with what was mentioned earlier as the 'liberalism of neutrality.' Soft relativism holds that 'moral positions are not in any way grounded in reason or the nature of things but are ultimately just adopted by each of us because we find ourselves drawn to them.'[69]

If we recall our opening discussion, one of the criticisms of the culture of authenticity was its apparent relativism with respect to what is the good life. Taylor is very aware of the possible slide towards a destructive form of subjectivism. To counter this possibility, he suggests a recovery of something analogous to what Rousseau has named *le sentiment de l'existence.* As we recall, Rousseau 'immensely enlarged the scope of the inner voice. We now can know from within us, from the impulses of our own being, what nature marks as significant.'[70] If part of the drive towards authenticity involves a recovery of this moral sentiment, its integration into our ideal of authenticity is necessary to avoid the slide into moral relativism. This inner moral feeling must be understood as something that connects us to a wider whole,[71] to something greater than ourselves. To have a sense that we are connected to a wider whole suggests that when the discussion pivots upon choice and self-constitution, we must be acutely aware that some options are more significant than others. Without a sense of connection to something greater than our own self- interest, the very idea of constituting ourselves according to some ideal will fall into triviality and hence incoherence. Without a sense of urgency and significance surrounding our choices, choosing vanilla ice cream as opposed to chocolate and choosing to tell the truth versus lying are on par with one another. Clearly this is absurd. Self-choice makes sense only because some issues are more important than others; it must presuppose that some choices are better than others, with the obverse also being true – that a particular choice may not be consonant with the ideal that orients our lives and hence our decisions. Thus any coherent conversation about 'self-choice' must always address the question what is it that we intend by our choices and decisions.

For Taylor, the question of why we have chosen this particular good or value as opposed to others, cannot be settled according to a criterion. From Taylor's perspective, *criteria* suggest that we follow a set of rules or a natural science methodology. The problem with this way of thinking about our choices is that it militates against the fact that our account of the world is 'essentially that of an embodied agent, engaged with or at grips with the world.'[72] To see practical reason as rule-following is to place the criterion outside lived experience. It also leads to moral scepticism, as practical reason is seen as something along the lines of Cartesian clarity and distinctness.[73] In other words, to give an account of our choice about what is good or valuable or our overarching hypergood is to engage in an act of practical reasoning that Taylor calls the *best account principle.* This form of practical reasoning is a hermeneutics of engagement. It is the way in which we try to make sense of our lives. Practical reasoning is not utilitarian, nor is it a form of naturalism, whereby we must get at the criteria for our decisions. Utilitarianism, because of its claim to be scientific, attempts to do away with 'qualitative distinctions of worth on grounds that they represent confused perceptions of the real bases of our preferences which are quantitative.'[74] This is a method of calculus. Utilitarianism is meant to be the solution to the challenge of naturalism. Naturalism arises in the context of the seventeenth-century Enlightenment cover story concerning the nature of science: science is about necessity and absolutes. Thus 'naturalism and the critical temper together tend to force us to recognize the apodictic mode as the only game in town.'[75] Rather, practical reasoning is a reasoning about transitions from one position A to new position B. Practical reasoning 'aims to establish, not that some position is correct absolutely, but rather that some position is superior to some other.'[76] Practical reasoning, therefore, is concerned with comparative evaluations: 'we show one of these comparative claims to be well founded when we can show that the *move* from A to B constitutes a gain epistemically.'[77] To gain epistemically means that a transition argument is an error-reducing argument. I come to realize that my earlier account of, say, justice was excessively narrow. The shift from position A to position B posits the claim that position B is the superior and more valid account, because I have gained greater purchase on the meaning of this term both culturally and individually. This claim is not the result of following rules or some other external criteria. In other words, transitional arguments, which are comparative claims about the true worth of competing values, have their 'source in biographical narrative.'[78] Rather, 'we are convinced that a certain view is superior because we have *lived* a transition which we understand as error-reducing and hence as epistemic gain'[79] (my emphasis). This epistemic gain is more than a mere addition of something to the one who is choosing. In every moral choice we are choosing to be a particular kind of person. This choosing of ourselves in the light of what now appears to be a truer good 'brings about a reversal which can be called a transfiguration.'[80] This reversal comes about through what Taylor calls a crisis of affirmation concerning what we have heretofore believed to be true, good, or morally worthwhile. The experience of a transfiguration of our vision[81] is a tacit account of moral conversion, and hence an act of human authenticity. We seek to take a new stand towards ourselves and the world.[82] This is not to suggest that transition claims are immune to further clarification. 'Our conviction that we have grown morally can be challenged by another. It may, after all, be illusion. And then we argue; and arguing here is contesting between interpretations of what I have been living.'[83]

If, in the context of the struggle to be authentic, higher goods arise so as to revalue earlier commitments, 'the conviction they carry comes from our reading of the transitions to them, from a certain understanding of moral growth.'[84] One of the issues at stake here in this transition to higher goods is the account of the order of argument. In a faulty form of moral reasoning we invoke realities that stand outside the context of the disputed interpretations. We start with something like 'the Good' or God and then work our way back to what ought to be done.[85] The problem with this approach is not with the Good or God. Rather it is the assumption that these higher goods stand outside the context of a lived narrative. Any discussion of higher goods, or moral ontology in general, must be given in 'anthropocentric terms, terms which relate to the meanings things have for us, then the demand to start outside of all such meanings, not to rely on our moral intuitions or on what we find morally moving, is in fact a proposal to change the subject.'[86] Certainly there is nothing preventing us from seeing God or the Good as foundational to our understanding of our self and our world. But our acceptance of any higher good is not because it stands outside or is independent of our lived moral experience. Rather, our apprehension of the worthwhileness of a particular higher good is grounded in a complex experience of being *moved* by it. This experience is somewhat analogous to what Eric Voeglin has described as the experience of pulls (*helkein*) and counter-pulls (*anthelkein*). The one invites to life and light, the other to darkness and death.[87] 'We sense in the very experience of being moved by some higher good that we are moved by what is good in it rather than that it is valuable because of our reaction. We are moved by seeing its point as something infinitely valuable. We experience our love for it as a well-founded love. Nothing that couldn't move me in *this* way would count as a hypergood.'[88] Again as with any good or value, the question of whether we are right or not is predicated upon whether we raise the relevant questions and face this or that particular critique.[89] Taylor eschews any discussion of criteria, which he associates with naturalism and utilitarianism, for a moral ontology that is anthropocentric. 'The most reliable moral view is not one that would be grounded quite outside our intuitions but one that is grounded on our strongest intuitions, where these have successfully met the challenge of proposed transitions away from them.'[90]

A significant element in Taylor's moral ontology is *phronesis* – practical reasoning. Practical reason properly understood, however, is not a view from nowhere. For Taylor, *phronesis* is closely associated with Aristotle's *aletheuein* – living in the truth.[91] Practical reason is more than moral formalism, or following a rule. 'What is considered right, in which we affirm or deny in the judgment about ourselves or about others, follows our general notions of what is good and right; still it only attains in the concrete reality of the case.'[92] Taylor's account of practical reason takes seriously the demands for ethical judgments. These ethical judgments are hermeneutical, acts of self-clarification about what we wish to be, and the context in which we find ourselves. Moreover, 'this context stands as the unexplicated horizon within which – or to vary the image, as the vantage point out of which – this experience can be understood.'[93] Engaged agency means that we find ourselves (individually as well as culturally) within a lived 'background' of past value judgments. This background is what makes all of our choices intelligible. However, as a background it is analogous to Heidegger's notion of 'pre-understanding.' 'To bring it to articulacy is to take (some of) this and make it explicit.'[94] Lastly, to ask what is the good that we are choosing in a given situation is to find ourselves situated within an already constituted background conversation about what this good might be. This, then, leads us to further ask what Taylor understands as the good.

Some postmodernists see goods and values as mere projections of wants and desires, and by implication optional, such as John Rawls who approaches the question of social relationships in terms of what it is right to do, rather than what it is good to be.[95] Taylor takes a much different stance. For him the question of our identity, and thus our authenticity, is intimately linked to the issue of the good. Our identity – our sense of self – is very much tied to how we see ourselves fitting into a whole and the direction that this may take.[96] Taylor maintains that one of the most basic aspirations of all of us is to be connected to something greater than ourselves. We desire to be in contact with what we see 'as good, or of crucial importance, or of fundamental value. This orientation to the good is essential to being a functional human agent.'[97] Taylor finds in all of us, then, an aspiration to fullness, to completeness.[98] One may say there is in our very being an erotic desire to be in union with something greater than ourselves, so as to be complete. In contradistinction to Heidegger, who sees authenticity as ultimately rooted in the disintegration of our being in death, Taylor understands authenticity as an orientation to and a desire to pattern our life after something greater: a higher meaning, greater story, or perhaps both. This patterning of our life around something greater brings about this longed for sense of fullness and completion.[99] For Taylor, it is not possible for human beings to be without an orientation to the good. It is not an option. What we hold to be valuable, important, or good gives us insight into what it means to live in the universe as a human being. 'The issue of our condition can never be exhausted for us by what we are, because we are also changing and becoming ... Since we cannot do without an orientation to the good, and since we cannot be indifferent to our place relative to this good, and since this place is something that must always change and become, the issue of the direction of our lives must rise for us.'[100]

Taylor is convinced that an orientation to the good is not something that we can do without because the direction of our lives is not static; in fact it is more properly understood in terms of 'becoming.'[101] Analogously, the good that orients us is also something not fully realized. The good that orients us and indicates the direction of our lives is something of a heuristic. Thus, my understanding of the good has to be woven into my developing understanding of my life as an unfolding story, a narrative.[102] Simply put, the shape of this good stands in relation to the unfolding narrative of our life. As a heuristic, the good can be 'some action, or motive, or style, which is seen as qualitatively superior. Good is used ... in a highly general sense, designating anything considered valuable, worthy, admirable, of whatever kind or category.'[103] It should not be assumed, however, that our vision of the good stands over and against our self-understanding. It seems that there is something of a symbiotic relationship between our vision of the good and our own self- understanding. How we see ourselves, the kind of person we are, determines the goods that shape our identity; nonetheless, our identity is structured and shaped by the goods that we choose to be important. There is a mutual shaping and structuring between our vision of the good and our self-understanding. There is an intimate relationship between our notion of the good and our understanding of the self. The narrative we use to give an account of our identity and the direction of our life is also intimately bound up with how we understand the good that is orienting us. 'So the issue for us has to be not only where we are, but where we're going ... That is why an absolute question always frames our relative ones.'[104] Finally, our notions of the good also express our conceptions of society and what it means to be an authentic human being acting in concert with other human beings.[105]

While the notion of the good may be heuristic, Taylor does make some crucial distinctions in order not to leave the discussion at such a general level. He introduces a distinction between 'constitutive' goods and 'life goods.'[106] A constitutive good is a good ordered to our actions and desires and is thereby used as a means to judge the moral worth of our actions. For example, love of God may be a constitutive good. It is a fundamental moral source and 'it is something the love of which empowers us to do and be good.'[107] Life goods, by contrast, are those qualitative distinctions we make between actions, feelings, and modes of life; these are the furniture of a good life, and these are seen as good because of their relationship to a constitutive good. Examples of certain life goods would be 'freedom, altruism, universal justice.'[108] While life goods are vital to living a 'good life,' constitutive goods shape our notion of authenticity. More importantly, love for the constitutive good 'empowers us to be good and loving it [the constitutive good] is part of what it is to be a good human being.'[109]

Hypergoods and Moral Reasoning

Another way to approach a constitutive good is to see it in terms of what Taylor calls a hypergood. 'Let me call higher-order goods of this kind 'hypergoods,' that is, goods that not only are incomparably more important than others but provide the standpoint from which these must be weighed, judged, and decided about.'[110] For most of us there is usually one highest good that orients and ranks all other goods. It is the orientation to this highest good that comes closest to defining my identity; therefore my direction to this good is of unique importance to me. 'The assurance that I am turned towards this good gives me a sense of wholeness, of fullness of being as a person or self, that nothing else can.'[111] This determines and shapes my notion of authenticity. Whatever hypergood moves me, it orders all other goods. So a hypergood is an architectonic good, an ideal that structures and shapes my sense of who and what I am. It brings about a trans-valuation of values. All previous values and goods are judged, ranked, and subsumed under this hypergood. However, Taylor is quick to point out that this trans-valuation is not immune to conflict and future revision: 'This transvaluation is not a once and for all affair – the older condemned goods remain, resist and struggle and tension continues.'[112] What becomes crucial is that our hypergood (our ideal) be large enough to combine 'to the greatest possible degree all the goods we seek.'[113]

Of course, whenever any discussion of hypergoods arises, what immediately comes to mind is the neo-Nietzschean critique of such goods. The critique usually suggests that hypergoods are 'cover stories for various forms of social exclusion and domination.'[114] Yet Taylor masterfully and quite accurately shows that even these postmodern critiques of any notion of a hypergood are themselves 'heavily overdetermined.'[115] They also are grounded in a vision of an orienting good that structures their own identity and decisions. Whether it is a modern notion of freedom, or universal dignity, or equality, neo-Nietzschean critiques cannot escape falling into a performative contradiction.[116] The real issue is not whether hypergoods are cover stories for oppression, for they have been (and this equally applies to the postmodernist who fails to advert to what hypergood orients his or her own operations). This failure itself also leads to a form of oppression – the silencing of major questions. What is at stake is not hypergoods per se, but the realization that we are all, in one way or another, moved by an orienting ideal that does transcend us. This orienting ideal constitutes what it means for us to be authentic. Yet it is clear that more often than not this ideal of authenticity remains unthematized, somewhat inchoate, if we are to properly and reasonably address the question of authenticity, what is called for is 'articulation.' It is only in what Taylor calls 'articulation' – making explicit what is implicit – that the discussion concerning the notion of authenticity can bear fruit.

'To give a certain articulation is to shape our sense of what we desire or what we hold important in a certain way.'[117] Something is important individually or culturally only to the degree it is expressed through acts of meaning. What is vital, significant can exist for us only through articulation. Only through expressing just what the community holds dear, or for that matter what we consider to be most important, can we come closer to 'the good as a moral source.' To fail to articulate what goods structure our choices and decisions is in large measure to surrender our freedom and responsibility for being the type of person we wish to be. 'Articulating our qualitative distinctions is setting out the point of our moral actions.'[118] Articulation is an attempt to formulate what is most important to us; what is most important moves us to be faithful to something that transcends the self.[119] But determining what this 'something' is requires that we look at another activity that is bound up in the act of articulation: the power of evaluation.

One of the distinguishing characteristics of being human is our power to evaluate our desires. Our self-understanding is very much tied to this power of evaluation.[120] The capacity to discriminate with respect to our feelings and desires helps us to clarify what we consider important and worthwhile. Without this ability we would be at the mercy of our passions, and none of our choices would emanate from a position of freedom. In Taylor's view this capacity for evaluation pivots between weak and strong evaluations. A weak evaluation tends more to be concerned with the outcome of a particular choice. For example, Taylor, in his essay 'What Is Human Agency?' uses the situation of choosing a vacation to show the nature of weak evaluations: 'I choose a holiday in the south rather than the north ... the favoured alternative is not selected because of the worth of the underlying motivation. There is 'nothing to choose' between the motivations here ... What is missing in this case is a distinction between the desires as to worth, and that is why it is not a strong evaluation.'[121] A strong evaluation is more interested in the quality of our motivation. We are trying to distinguish whether our desires are worthy of being pursued.[122] Thus strong evaluations orbit around such terms as *noble/base* and *courageous/cowardly*. When we speak of strong evaluations we make reference to goods or values that are incomparable. 'There are ends or goods which are worthy or desirable in a way that cannot be measured on the same scale as our ordinary ends, goods.'[123] This is to suggest that these ends or goods are standards by which we judge our desires, decisions, and choices. In short, to distinguish between strong evaluations and weak evaluations is to contrast the different type of self that each evaluation involves: 'Motivations or desires do not only count in virtue of the attraction of the consummations but also in virtue of the kind of life and kind of subject that these desires properly belong to.'[124] This, by implication, is the question of authenticity.

As stated previously, strong evaluations – hermeneutical judgments – seek to distinguish between desires that are noble and base. Such terms are grounded in a vision of a life that expresses and sustains it. To quote Taylor, 'To characterize one desire or inclination as worthier, or nobler than others is to speak of it in terms of the kind of quality of life which it expresses and sustains.'[125] To reiterate, authenticity means that for each of us there is one unique way for each of us to-be-in-the-world. Authenticity is an ideal that structures my life, whereby I choose to do what I ought to do, rather than merely what I want to do. From this understanding of authenticity, I can see the importance attached to Taylor's distinction between weak and strong evaluations. For it is only within this context that I am able to truly understand what it is that motivates *my* choices. The capacity for evaluation through articulation enables me to understand the goods that shape my choices. Is there one good or ideal that is an architectonic good whereby all of my other choices are ordered to that one Ideal? What kind of a person do I wish to be? And how does this ideal orient the fundamental choices towards bringing that about?

There is one last point concerning this capacity for evaluation. Taylor insists that mere choice is not the criterion for judging what is worthwhile or not. Just because we choose something does not automatically make that choice worthwhile, valuable, good, or in line with what it means to be authentic. Mere choice, or 'decisionism,' denies any ordering of goods and priorities and makes all choices of equal worth. As we saw earlier, decisionism leads to the absurd conclusion that choosing ice cream is as worthwhile as deciding to sacrifice one's life for the sake of another. 'In order to speak of choice, we cannot just find ourselves in one of the alternatives. We have in some sense to experience the pull of each and give our assent to one.'[126] This experience is part of the normativity to right choosing. We must have a deep and abiding sense of the difference between strong and weak evaluation. Not only do strong evaluations focus upon what we consider to be truly worthwhile, but also we identify with those convictions.[127] To do violence to these types of evaluations constitutes an act of self-mutilation. This is why the capacity for articulation and evaluation is so important. 'To give a certain articulation is to shape our sense of what we desire or what we hold important in a certain way.'[128] Articulation not only helps us to better discriminate between competing desires, but it is also vital in helping us delineate what it means for each of us to be authentic: what kind of person do I wish to be, and what is the good or ideal that orients my life, and how do my decisions reflect it? Lastly, Taylor is critical regarding subjectivism and its attendant epistemological claims. In addition, the old cosmological order, and its understanding of human nature, is no longer viable. Does this then place Taylor in a situation in which the questions about the truth of human existence are merely a matter of opinion? If this is indeed the case, then the question of epistemology itself should, as Rorty suggests, 'be something we should put behind us.'[129] Taylor, however, is not given to this form of epistemological despair. Drawing upon Heidegger, Taylor understands the dialogical nature of the person as normative. This is so because even in 'our theoretical stance to the world we are (intentional) agents. Even to find out about the world and formulate disinterested pictures, we have to come to grips with it, experiment, set ourselves to observe, control conditions ... we are engaged as agents coping with things.'[130]

The normative task of human reason, as engaged agency, is to be reasonable. It is to be conversationally attentive to the need to articulate 'the background, disclosing what it involves.'[131] In short, epistemological realism means for Taylor to be able to articulate degrees of differences in value claims, and more significantly that 'we are able to show that the passage from one (value claim) to the other represents a gain in understanding.'[132]

Epiphany as a Moral Source

Up to this point, much of our conversation has focused on the questions of identity and authenticity, and how important articulation and evaluation are in truly clarifying the goods and values that move us and structure our choices. Yet the question still remains, whether this discussion about goods and hypergoods also falls into the trap of soft relativism. Is the self the sole locus for determining what constitutes authenticity, or are there horizons of meaning independent of us that enable us to truly discover what it means to be an authentic human being? Taylor wants to argue that 'our normal understanding of self-realization presupposes that some things are important beyond the self, that there are some goods or purposes the furthering of which has significance for us and which can provide significance for us and which can provide the significance a fulfilling life needs.'[133] Yet we must still ask how we determine or discover what is most important in shaping our identity, in articulating our ideal of authenticity. Is there a source other than my self?

To answer these questions, Taylor introduces the notion of epiphany. An epiphany is the 'manifestation which brings us into the presence of something which is otherwise inaccessible, and which is of the highest moral or spiritual significance.'[134] The notion of epiphany helps to address the question of where we discover moral sources that reside outside us. The idea of a framing epiphany is critical if we are to avoid certain restrictive and potentially dangerous approaches to human agency. In *Sources of the Self*, Taylor shows how the modern turn to the subject and the breakdown of an older order of meaning left the human subject adrift; he no longer lived within the context of a world of agreed-upon meanings. With the passing of this hierarchical order, the subject was thrown back upon herself, disembedded, and left with the burden of determining what is meaningful.

This breakdown of the medieval synthesis gave rise to two distinct approaches that sought to fill the gap in human meaning: expressive subjectivism and instrumental reason. Expressive subjectivism, as we stated at the beginning of this chapter, maintains that we discover what is most worthwhile in the depths of our own being. Again, Rousseau's *sentiment de l'existence* exemplifies this descent within to discover what is of utmost importance. Yet clearly this expressive subjectivism also has its dark side: the moral and spiritual can become pure constructs of the individual's expressivism. Subjective fulfilment becomes tied to what I consider to be good, and this evaluation is severed from any other considerations outside my personal vision of self-fulfilment.

If, however, expressive subjectivism leads to a pernicious form of individualism, the rise of the notion of instrumental reason further exacerbates the problem, but in a very different way. It is not necessary to repeat Taylor's analysis of how reason becomes understood as instrumental. What is important is the fact that reason is seen more in the light of a tool that functions with respect to a means-end relationship, rather than a normative activity of the person that allows us to raise and answer questions concerning what it truly means to be authentic. In other words, instrumental reason restricts the horizon of questions that we can ask to the point that decisions and choices are already circumscribed by predetermined criteria. In *The Ethics of Authenticity* Taylor specifies how instrumental reason can severely cripple economic choices. If a certain bottom-line mentality is the measure for choices, then questions about the impact on individuals, families, and communities are deemed irrelevant. Issues that fall outside of this limited perspective are thought worthless. This is why the question of a framing epiphany becomes so crucial for Taylor.[135] The notion of a framing epiphany overcomes the relativism and the instrumentalization of human reason, by revealing to the human agent meanings and values that transcend the limitations of self-concern, or the utilitarian understanding of reason.

In order for Taylor to clarify what he means by a framing epiphany, he turns to the rise of modern art and poetry. Modern art and poetry together articulate the importance of the subjective expressivism without falling into subjectivism. Taylor sees in modern poetry the potential to show us a particular moral or spiritual order while being indexed to a personal vision.[136] Again, authenticity is 'clearly self-referential: this has to be my orientation. But this doesn't mean that on another level the content must be self-referential.'[137] Modern art and poetry can steer us between the threats of Charybdis and Scylla. Taylor does not deny that subjective fulfilment is a good, but this fulfilment must 'be part of a package, to be sought within a life which is also aimed at other goods.'[138] Again it is a proper understanding of an epiphany that can open us up to fuller insights into authenticity. As Taylor makes clear, 'realizing an epiphany is a paradigm case of what I have called discovery contact with a moral source.'[139] Because we now live in an age in which 'a publicly accessible cosmic order of meaning'[140] is no longer possible, the idea of epiphany bridges the gap that has been left with this disintegration of public order. The idea of an epiphany anchors Taylor's concern with the search 'for moral sources *outside* the subject through languages which resonate *within* him or her, the grasping of an order which is inseparably indexed to a personal vision.'[141] A great epiphanic work of art, or an encounter with nature,[142] can not only place us in contact with the 'source it taps. It can realize the contact.'[143] Taylor finds the poetry of Rainer Maria Rilke to be a paradigmatic example of epiphanic art. Rilke shows us that 'the world is not simply an ensemble of objects for our use, but makes a further claim on us ... And this demand, though connected with what we are as language beings is not simply one of self-fulfillment. It emanates from the world.'[144] An epiphanic event then fosters or constitutes something that is not only spiritually significant but also fulfils the desire for wholeness. It is a question of realism. In other words, art 'opens up a field of interrogation, but one of great importance if we want to understand ourselves.'[145]

Lastly, even though the poet's vision is personal, it is still a vision that is indexed to an object beyond himself. 'The epiphanic is genuinely mysterious, and it possibly contains the key – or a key – to what it is to be human.'[146] The central nature of epiphany is not just one's praxis, but also the intimate transactions that take place between one's self and one's world.[147] The desire to be authentic, to be truly self-fulfilled, is a call that is not only inward but also from the 'beyond.'[148] Or perhaps we might sum up what Taylor is trying to do by quoting Rilke:

> But because to be here means so very much.
> Because this fleeting sphere appears to needs us –
> in some strange way concerns us: we ... most fleeting of all.
> Once and once only for each thing – then no more.
> For us as well. Once. Then no more ... ever.
> But to have been as one, though but the once,
> with this world, never can be undone.[149]

After reading Taylor one certainly comes away with the sense that his 'truly being here is so much.' He has with great passion given us not only a portrait of our modern self, but has with great care retrieved what he thinks is best about modernity's notion of authenticity without turning a blind eye to its more aberrant expressions. Taylor embraces modernity and its quest for self-realization, and its concomitant freedom, not with a naive romanticism, but with a belief that a proper understanding of what lies beneath the 'jargon of authenticity' can help to raise the conversation above the two mutually exclusive positions of the 'boosters and knockers.' Borrowing from Pascal, Taylor sees modernity characterized by grandeur as well as by *misère*. 'Only a view that embraces both can give us the undistorted insight into our era that we need to rise to its greatest challenge.'[150] Taylor has given us such a view.

There is another thinker who has much in common with Taylor, who can also help us rise to the challenge of modernity's grandeur and *misère*. this thinker is the much-neglected Jesuit philosopher and theologian Bernard Lonergan. It is to the thought of Bernard Lonergan that we now turn.

3

Bernard Lonergan:
On Being Oneself

Whoever does not know how to find the way to his ideal lives more frivolously and impudently than the man without an ideal.

— Friedrich Nietzsche, *Beyond Good and Evil*

'On January 9, 1919 Heidegger himself wrote to (Fr.) Krebs ... explaining that "over the last two years I have struggled for a basic clarification of my philosophical position ... [However] epistemological insights extending to the theory of historical knowledge have made the *system* of Catholicism problematic and unacceptable to me."'[1] What Heidegger meant by the 'Catholic system' was a 'Romanized control of meaning through ahistorical orthodoxy.'[2] For Bernard Lonergan, this ahistorical orthodoxy, a 'classical mentality,' was the result of the church's failure to come to grips with modern science and Nietzsche's great insight about the historicity of human existence: 'historical mindedness.'[3] As Fred Lawrence explains,

> Lonergan's response to this problem was hermeneutic. It involved a
> critical acceptance of modern history and modern science ... Coming
> critically to terms with human facticity and historicity, he transposed
> his earlier groundbreaking interpretation of Aquinas's thought on
> grace and freedom in his 1972 work, *Method in Theology*. For Lonergan
> the integrity of method as hermeneutic demonstrates that in the
> post-modern (or any) era, science, scholarship, philosophy, and the-
> ology can only be genuine in the measure that they 'head one into
> being authentically human.'[4]

The Drama of Human Existence

For Lonergan, authentic existence is self-transcendence, and self-transcendence involves intellectual, moral, and religious conversion. However, to recall our account of Adorno's *Jargon of Authenticity*, two of his many criticisms levelled against the notion of authenticity are that it is elitist and that it diminishes the role of religion. It is elitist because the term seems to suggest that only a chosen few are called to rise above the day-to-day groaning of human existence and live a much more 'authentic life,' a life that by implication is richer, deeper, in essence more humanly profound than ordinary human living. It diminishes religion because the jargon of authenticity seems to be its own sacred calling. There are the 'Authentic Ones,' to use Adorno's phrase, and these substitute for the authority of God the 'absolutized authority' of their own claim to being authentic persons. Yet for Bernard Lonergan, the question of human authenticity is neither elitist nor a substitute for religion. Simply put, 'man achieves authenticity in self-transcendence.'[5] To live an authentic life is not for the chosen few; it is what we all must do if we are indeed to fully realize our own humanity. This means that we must also address the religious dimension of human existence. Authenticity is a life lived within the context of this threefold conversion. But as Lonergan is quick to point out, conversion is not a single and definitive achievement. 'Besides conversions there are breakdowns. What has been built up so slowly and so laboriously by the individual, the society, the culture, can collapse.'[6] Authenticity is a lifelong commitment, both individually and culturally, to the imperatives to be attentive, reasonable, intelligent, and responsible; in short, authenticity is a life that is intelligent, moral, and religious; it is properly a human way of life.

Just as for Taylor, Lonergan's initial approach in addressing what human authenticity means is hermeneutical. For Lonergan, the question of authentic human existence does not pivot upon a set of abstract propositions concerning what it means to be a person, nor is the discussion to be reduced to some limited and narrow vision of humanity, such as sociobiology. Rather, the person and the question of authenticity are concrete and specific; the question of what it means to be an authentic person refers to an individual with all of her encompassing characteristics. It is the question about the truth of human existence. The person is not an abstraction; she is a concrete reality, 'a being in the luminousness of being.'[7]

If the person is a 'being in the luminousness of being,' then our starting point in the question of authenticity will be the subject as he exists in the here and now: the over-all context of human living, the person as being-in-the-world. Lonergan likens our being-in-the-world, human existence, to a

drama. Human living is a drama because the person is ultimately concerned with more than merely getting things accomplished. She wants to
have a sense that there is direction to her living, and meaning to her
actions. As Lonergan states, 'Behind palpable activities, there are motives
and purposes; and in them it is not difficult to discern an artistic or more
precisely a dramatic component.'[8] Not only is the person 'capable of aesthetic liberation and artistic creativity, but his first work of art is his own living.'[9] Human existence is a dramatic enterprise that embraces all aspects
of human living – personal, communal, ethical, and religious – and it
unfolds in time; it is within this temporal unfolding of the dramatic enterprise that our understanding of the ideal of what it means to be a person
continues to shift and change. Lonergan, like Heidegger and Taylor,
understands that the being of the person and the drama that she lives out
is always contextualized; one's being is being-in-the-world. Taylor understands our being-in-the-world in terms of the 'engaged subject': 'the
human subject is an engaged agent, a subject ... who exists in the space of
subjective experience, descriptions, and self-interpretations.'[10] Lonergan's
notion of being-in-the-world is the concrete unfolding of human *Existenz*,
and *Existenz* is an all-encompassing category that expresses the sense of
being one's self[11] in all of its complexities and in all of its relationships. It is
at once 'psychological, sociological, historical, philosophic, theological,
religious, ascetic, perhaps for some even mystical; but it is all of them
because the person is all and involved in all.'[12] The person, then, is an
embodied and engaged entity, which means that she is embedded in time
and eventually subject to death. The fragility of the human drama reinforces the fact that 'we live and die, love and hate, rejoice and suffer,
desire, fear, wonder and dread, inquire and doubt,'[13] and pray.

If our being-in-the-world is this complex sense of being embedded in
time and ultimately subject to death, as Heidegger so clearly showed, then
there might be more to our being-in-the-world than mere concern with
practical matters. Given the contingency of our existence, we are perforce
burdened with being what it is that we wish to make of ourselves. Yet we
find ourselves caught within a certain tension that is inherent in the
drama. On the one hand, there seems to be an aspiration for transcendence and wholeness; but on the other there is the encounter with limitation and frailty that ultimately ends in death. We find ourselves
constrained by a certain givenness to our very being; and while it is true
that human living is both artistic and dramatic, unlike a work of art, however, we find ourselves limited in how we may shape ourselves. For
instance, one finds oneself already constituted biologically in a particular
way. Again, the self that we think we are is in large measure de-centred,
which means that our identity is to a large degree the product of a multi-

faceted process of socialization. The already given, the already constituted serves as the material used to shape our drama; it is in this already constituted horizon of meanings and values that the drama of human living unfolds.

Again drawing upon the work of Heidegger, Lonergan acknowledges that an important element constitutive of dramatic living is a sense of one's own 'thrownness' (*Geworfenheit*). The person finds herself already immersed within an ongoing drama that is already structured by a particular horizon of meanings and values. And as with any drama, there is for each one of us an underlining vision that shapes the whole of our concrete living. All aspects of our lives are shaped by, more often than not, an unthematized ideal or set of ideals that order all our choices and decisions. In other words, dramatic living is a pattern shaped and formed by an image or ideal of what it means to be a human being. The source of this ideal, or ideals, which is both individual and communal, remains largely unthematized, and quite often the ideals can be conflictual.[14]

In Taylor this unthematized context is the notion of background. For Lonergan, it is a foreground already constituted by others and given over as the point from which I am to decide what I wish to be as a person. Another term that Lonergan, Taylor, and Heidegger use for the givenness of this foreground is *horizon*. We all live out the drama of our lives within a horizon that is both constituted and constituting. It is constituted because it is an already given set of judgments and decisions – judgments and decisions that are both personal and communal; it is constituting because it is the context from which the subject continues to make choices, decisions, and judgments concerning one's being-in-the-world. My horizon is the boundary of what I know and value. Anything outside of that boundary does not exist for me. 'What we know and how we arrange our scale of values determines our horizons and our horizons determine the range of our attention, our consideration, our valuations, our conduct.'[15] A horizon is the world of our interests, and it is that place in which we live out our lives, and it is fixed or bounded by the 'range of our interests and our knowledge.'[16] It is in horizon analysis that Lonergan draws heavily upon Heidegger's notion of *Sorge*. It is one's *Sorge* (concern) that determines what our horizon will be, which is to say, 'all human knowing [I would add valuing and loving] occurs within a context, a horizon, a total view, an all-encompassing framework ... and apart from that context it loses sense, significance, meaning.'[17] The shape of our horizon is directly proportional to our care, *Sorge*. In other words, what I am concerned with, what I love will be integrated within my horizon. Those meanings and values that reside outside my caring do not exist for me; they are outside my horizon of concern.

To repeat, human living is a drama that encompasses the whole of human living; we experience ourselves as embodied, which means that the dramatic pattern of human existence does not dismiss the biological exigencies that are also part of concrete human existence. Rather, given proper representation, even these biological demands may be transformed and integrated into higher levels of meaning.[18] For example, we do not merely eat in order to fulfil a biological need. This exigency can be transformed by a particular ideal and integrated into a social context in which eating becomes dining, and dining is an activity for lovers, family, and friends. The act of dining with others moves the biological need for food to a higher level of meaning in which this exigency can be satisfied and integrated within a nexus of other related desires. For example, Leon Kass, in *The Hungry Soul*, writes, 'Eating can also be an expression of our personal humanity, indeed of excellence or virtue. As in other matters the social setting becomes a stage on which individuals display their characters, virtuous or not.'[19]

Again, the dramatic pattern is more than just concern for the practical aspects of organized living; it is structured around the insight that we are ultimately responsible for the types of people we are and hope to be. It is within the context of the dramatic pattern that the question of what constitutes authentic human existence arises, for the drama of human living is not just a matter of memorizing roles and the proper responses to them. It is also more than developing the necessary skills to cope with the requirements of practical human living. Dramatic living means that we live in a world mediated by meaning and motivated by value. Moreover, whether we are explicitly aware of it or not, each of us is burdened with the task of deciding what type of person we wish to be in the context of the drama that is our life. It is in the dramatic pattern that 'insights emerge and accumulate that govern the imaginative projects of dramatic living.'[20] To repeat, ordinary living is not simply ordinary drama. While it is true that there is a certain givenness to our role, nonetheless, what is allowed into consciousness is already patterned, and this pattern is emotionally shaped by what *we find* to be most worthwhile, valuable, and interesting.[21]

Yet what we find to be most worthwhile and most valuable can be problematic. Just as Heidegger spoke of 'idle chatter and curiosity' as ways in which Dasein inoculates itself against the truth of its own existence, so Lonergan speaks about how we can pervert or distort the drama in which we are involved. Just as insights are desired in order to ensure the smooth flow of human living, insights that might upset this flow can be unwanted. Just as the prisoner in Plato's allegory of the cave escaped and fell in love with the Light, so those prisoners left behind continued to be in love with darkness. There exists, then, the possibility of either raising or suppressing questions, desiring to know the truth or fleeing from that possibility by refusing to raise questions and hence the unwanted insights. This Lonergan calls the problem of dramatic bias. Dramatic bias is an aberration of the understanding, or a *scotosis*, a 'blind spot.'[22] *Scotosis* lies below the level of thematized awareness. 'It arises, not in conscious acts, but in the censorship that governs the emergence of psychic contents.'[23] A *scotosis* restricts the ability to understand ourselves and others. It occludes any new avenues of understanding that may call into question the contrast between what we claim to be and what we are. In other words, this 'blind spot' will allow insights to emerge, but if the insight appears to be challenging or threatening to the subject's psychic security, it will be rationalized away, ignored, or repressed. What develops is a subject split between what Lonergan terms the 'persona' (the public self) and the 'ego' (the private self).[24] The split in the subject is exacerbated by the fact that the healthy function of what Freud calls the censor has become aberrant.[25] Normally the censorship is constructive: 'it selects and arranges materials that emerge in consciousness in a perspective that gives rise to an insight.'[26] These insights help us to shape our identity vis-à-vis an orienting ideal. Thus the censor is both positive and negative. The negative aspect of its function means that certain materials and perspectives that are irrelevant to the wanted insight are not brought to light.[27] However, when the censor is functioning improperly, any positive materials that would give rise to unwanted insights that would call into question our 'persona' are prevented from arising within consciousness.[28] The activity of repression then becomes the dominating mode of the censor: what are repressed are unwanted insights. Moreover, because insights arise from images, to prevent unwanted insights means that we inhibit the demands for images. Thus insights are 'unwanted, not because they confirm our current viewpoints and behaviour, but because they lead to their correction and revision.'[29]

The Existential Gap and Conversion

As stated previously, all of us live out our existence in the context of a world, a horizon, and this horizon is the sum total of what matters most to us – our concern, Heidegger's *Sorge*. 'It [*Sorge*] determines the horizon within which lies our world, our potential totality of objects.'[30] Put another way, '*Dasein* is being-in-the-world, and this being-in-the-world is a function of one's concern.'[31] To state the obvious, this horizon will be limited, for it is only as large as the area of our concern. All of our thinking and doing concerning what it means to be a human being operates under the constraints of a horizon.[32] Thus in a situation of personal or social decline, we will miss possible remedies because of the limitation of a particular horizon. 'They'll be looking for all kinds of remedies and cures and ways of fixing things up but the one thing necessary is what they'll miss and they'll miss it because their thinking is within the limitation of a given horizon.'[33] Because our horizon is the boundary and limit to our existence, to our world, there is a real resistance to moving beyond the familiar and accessible.[34] Our horizon may allow us to navigate somewhat freely in the world because it is a synthesis for successful living. Who and what we are and how we are situated in the larger drama of our lives are defined within this horizon, and to find ourselves in conflict with our world view, with what we value most, and our sense of self-understanding, produces a sense of dread and a real confrontation with death. To raise the question of whether I am what I claim to be, or whether my real world is *the* real world becomes extremely difficult.

> To move beyond one's horizon in any significant fashion involves
> reorganization of the subject, a reorganization of modes of living,
> feeling, thinking, judging, desiring, fearing, willing, deliberating,
> choosing. Against such reorganization of the patterns of the subject,
> there come into play all the conservative forces that give our lives
> their continuity and their coherence. The subject's fundamental anx-
> iety, his deep distress, is over the collapse of himself and his world;
> tampering with the organization of himself gives rise to dread.[35]

Thus we may find ourselves in a situation in which our 'world' conflicts with the relative horizon of society; we encounter what was already detailed earlier – our *thrownness*. Yet it is precisely the awareness that things are not working within a given horizon that gives rise to the possibility of discovering the means of moving beyond our limited position. This going beyond the limits of our horizon, the expansion of our interests and concerns coincides with the exigency of authenticity, which in turn raises the question of how we move from a limited horizon to a much fuller one, which is to raise the question of conversion.

There is, then, a fundamental problem to human living that is both personal and communal. It has to do with what Lonergan calls the 'existential gap,'[36] or what Taylor sees as the problem of transfiguration.[37] 'The existential gap is the gap between what we are overtly, and what exists covertly in what we are. We can repeat the words and not have the meaning because our horizon is not broad enough.'[38] The issue of conversion, then, resolves the question of what it means to be an authentic person, especially in light of this 'existential gap.' Conversion is a movement into a new horizon; it is a radical change in our orientation to the world, and this new orientation can reveal ever-greater depth, breadth, and wealth to the human drama. Conversion is a new understanding of one's self, and the key to a 'basic horizon.' It is only in terms of conversion that we are able to address whether we are indeed living truthfully, morally, and religiously. Conversion is foundational to any proper understanding of human existence.

Such a term as conversion, however, usually raises certain hesitations, if not strong resistance. For more often than not, the term is used in reference to a religious conversion. Yet it is that kind of reaction that points to the need to at least broach the subject. We know that conversion in the general sense is a movement to a new horizon; it not only involves a change in how we successfully live our lives,[39] but also expands what we consider most valuable and worthwhile. This change in how we concretely live out our life is ultimately a concern for the truth by which we live our lives; it is the truth involved in the choices we make in self-constitution.[40] Thus if we are interested in living a more truth-filled *Existenz*, a more truth-filled drama, we will need to broaden our horizon and this requires conversion. This is so because of an 'underlying problem and it is personal. Each of us has his or her world; it is a solid structure; it is the result of our lives; it has a horizon. And this world is apt to define what I mean by the real.'[41]

Because our horizons are always increments of 'the basic horizon,'[42] only through the dynamics of conversion – a conversion that is personal, communal, and historical, and a conversion that subsumes prior horizons without abolishing them – can the question of what it means to be an authentic person be adequately addressed.[43] For it is quite clear that our concept of what it means to be human 'determines fundamentally what kind of a technical, social, cultural situation people will be producing,'[44] and the results of this concept will be ongoing and cumulative. If, for example, a particular horizon systematically excludes questions concerning one's religious nature and what that might mean with respect to the polity, then one personally and collectively 'increases the evils in a given situation.'[45] Moreover, each concrete situation 'objectifies and reveals what man's thought about man has been, but it also suggests and motivates change in man's thinking about man,'[46] and this is the question of conversion.

Again, to reiterate, we find ourselves involved in a drama. The context of this dramatic enterprise means we seek to shape ourselves in order to fit a certain ideal that we have of what it means to be human. We have also seen how something like dramatic bias can pervert, restrict, or split what it means to be one's self. Yet we may ask the question, what does it mean to be one's self? What is this self that I claim to be at this moment and that I wish to be in the future? The self that Lonergan speaks of is a concrete reality that has been formed in and through the communities of which it has been a part, as well as its own decisions in terms of self-formation. For Lonergan, this self is the irreducible element in the person from which spring the decisions and choices of an authentic person, and the drifting and forgetting of the inauthentic person.[47] To put it another way, what the person is to make of himself depends upon what possibilities he will have; these possibilities are found within the context of culture, communal and personal relationships, human history, and ultimately with God.[48] Thus, the wider the possibilities, the greater the opportunity we will have in constituting ourselves with respect to a fuller, richer, and more adequate orienting ideal. Here Lonergan distinguishes between nature and subject. 'It is true that human nature is always the same; a man is a man whether he is awake or asleep, young or old, sane or crazy, sober or drunk ... a saint or a sinner.'[49] The human being is not, however, an abstraction. Drawing upon Augustine's truth of existence, 'the self is not a substance one unearths by peeling away layers until one gets to the core, but an integrity one struggles to bring into existence.'[50] For Lonergan, then, as for Taylor and Heidegger, 'the being of the subject is becoming. One becomes oneself.'[51] It is a question of development. If one is asleep and unconscious then one is still a human being but potentially a person. If one is at least dreaming then one is minimally a person; if one is awake and sensing, seeing, tasting, hearing, and so forth, then one is experientially a person. If one asks questions and begins to inquire, seeks to understand, and then makes judgments concerning what is true and real, one is being an intelligent and reasonable person. It is, however, when one begins to ask questions about what is truly worthwhile, what actually is the right way to live that one is existentially a person.[52]

The subject truly becomes existential when he discovers that it is up to him to decide what kind of person he wishes to be, what he wants to make of himself.[53] This discovery awakens the subject to one unavoidable fact; he is the one responsible for constituting himself through his various choices and decisions. Moreover, in accepting this burden of self-constitution, an individual must form some view of the universe and how his life is to unfold in the context of that Weltanschauung. However, as noted previously, one's ideas about what it means to be fully a person, more often than not, are first shaped by the 'situation in which he finds himself and secondly by the horizon in which he thinks about himself.'[54] Not only is the existential subject concerned with being a certain kind of person; he is primordially concerned with being the person he concretely is here and now.[55] Even for someone like Nietzsche, there is an exigency to being human. While he may be ambivalent about what this exigency truly is, still he makes 'room for the turbulent struggle for power and the Apollonian yearning for peace; speaking in the guise of Zarathustra, Nietzsche gives voice both to Promethean rebellion and to the quiet search for the *blessed isle.*'[56] Here again Lonergan and Taylor converge. Taylor gives us a thicker account of Rousseau's *sentiment de l'exist-*

ence as a way to overcome the flattening of human existence. Lonergan posits that *'l'homme se définit par une exigence,* man is defined not by some static essence that he has at first, but by an exigence, by a requirement'[57] to become something more than what he is at any given moment.

Authenticity as an Activity

Along with Taylor, Lonergan is clear there is a dynamic longing within the person for wholeness and completion. This erotic desire for wholeness can open the person up to the question, what kind of person do I wish to be? Again, to raise this question is for Lonergan the existential discovery. It is the awareness, albeit implicit, that I am incomplete within myself and that as an embodied being who is ultimately subject to death there is also this experience of *helkein* and *anthelkein*[58] – pulls and counter-pulls. One invites to life, the other to death. We saw with Taylor that this experience is associated with trying to give reasons for my choices. With Lonergan, it is this experience of the various pulls and counter-pulls that brings to light the fact that it is indeed I who must bear the burden of constituting myself to be a certain type of person. Through my decisions I make myself either someone in accordance with a particular ideal or someone who dramatically diverges from this ideal.[59] 'By my free acts I am making myself. The series of my choices gives me the character I have. One can say that all men have the same nature, but there is also a personal differentiation of one from the other, and this differentiation is grounded in the choices that one makes:'[60] to make choices, decisions, and take risks makes one an existential subject. Through our decisions, choices, and the risks taken we reveal ourselves to others. We reveal the type of person we are at the moment; we reveal the ideal that informs our way of living; we reveal what we consider to be worthwhile, true, real, and valuable in terms of human living. It is an 'original creation' that is revealed. But what is revealed is not a creation ex nihilo. The self that is revealed is the self that has been constituted through the orienting vision of our choices both past and present, and as a product of a multifaceted socialization.

> Freely the subject makes himself what he is; never in this life is the making finished; always it is still in process, always it is a precarious achievement that can slip and fall and shatter. Concern with subjectivity ... is concern with the intimate reality of man. It is concern not with the universal truths that hold whether a man is asleep or awake, not with the interplay of natural factors and determinants, but with the perpetual novelty of self-constitution, of free choices making the chooser what he is.[61]

We have spoken of the existential subject as someone who must make choices and decisions, and take risks in order to constitute himself in accordance with a particular ideal. Yet it would be a mistake to assume that all of us fall into the category of being an existential subject. There is the problem of the drifter. In the drifter individuality is blurred; he seeks to blend in with the crowd. What the crowd thinks, the drifter thinks. Like Heidegger's *das Man*, the drifter wants to be like everyone else.[62] Even in the drifter's cry of 'it's my choice,' 'what sounds like the assumption of ultimate responsibility is usually the flourish of moral retreat, the refusal to discuss, explain, and justify a decision and the retirement'[63] to anonymity. The drifter out of fear surrenders his freedom for a type of controlled living that appears to be secure and solid. Yet what the drifter fails to confront is that there is always an element of risk in his choice and decision, because he does not know everything about the situation he faces.[64] Our journey of self-discovery is more often than not in the night. The control that we have is always more or less; we must believe, risk, and dare if the drama that we live is to have any kind of direction.[65] In short, the drama of our life, our being-in-the-world, is always circumscribed by limits; there is the limit of a particular time and place in which we find ourselves; but over and above this fact there are the limits that intimately shape each and every one of us: death, struggle, guilt, and suffering. Even the drifter cannot escape the fact of death. No one can die for me. It is something that I must confront. These situations are not only profoundly personal, but they demand the total involvement of who and what we are and what we wish to be.[66] This is the question of authenticity.

The core of this question presupposes that there exists some horizon of significance independent of the person asking the question; otherwise the question would intend nothing, or the question would not even arise. This horizon of meaning should stand as something of a beacon; it would illuminate the person's question concerning whether she really is what she claims to be. For Lonergan, a question such as, am I really what I claim to be? is a question about what it means to be an authentic human being. This question about authenticity is all-inclusive, because it implies that the person is not just intellect or just a will. 'Though concerned with results, he or she more basically is concerned with himself or herself as becoming good or evil.'[67] She is concerned with the totality of what it means for her to be-in-the-world.

The notion of authenticity can be differentiated into two mutually determining elements. First there is what Lonergan terms the minor authenticity of the subject. This aspect is concerned with the tradition that nourishes the person, for example, the Hindu tradition. So the question, am I a good Hindu? intends its answer within the already given Hindu tradition. Again, one could say yes and be correct; on the other hand, one could answer in the affirmative and be mistaken. Thus, there will be elements from the tradition that coincide with the subject, and elements in the subject that diverge from that same tradition. The problem that arises with respect to the minor authenticity of the subject is that the person is usually unaware of the difference between what is claimed and what indeed is the fact. According to Lonergan, the person usually does not possess an adequately differentiated language with which to articulate what he truly is. What can happen, then, is that the subject will misuse the language of the tradition, thereby devaluing and distorting it, in order to appropriate this mistaken understanding of what that tradition is. If this distortion, however, takes place on a massive scale then one is faced with the issue of major authenticity. It is the inauthenticity of individuals that generates the inauthenticity of the traditions, and vice versa. If a tradition has indeed become corrupted, then what occurs is something of a tragedy, for a person can take only the current tradition and its norms as his standard; if these standards and norms have become debased, the subject tries to truthfully appropriate what has become corrupted or inauthentic. Thus a vicious cycle is perpetuated. The task that befalls any person who seeks his way out of this morass of inauthenticity is first to undo his own lapse in goodness, and this is a moment of conversion. Then he must proceed to discover what is corrupt about the tradition itself. In order to accomplish this act of retrieval vis-à-vis the tradition, questions need to be raised concerning how a particular tradition was formed and transmitted: this is the question of major authenticity.[68] Taylor's *Sources of the Self* is an outstanding example of this type of retrieval, or as Taylor might suggest, a recovery of our proper heritage.

To ask whether we are indeed what we claim to be is to raise the question about human authenticity. The notion of being an authentic person – someone who is trying to narrow the 'existential gap' – suggests that the question of authenticity really is about the ideal tendencies of the human spirit towards what is true, good, and worthwhile, as well as our spiritual longings.[69] These then are what truly constitute our fundamental orientation in the world, our *Sorge*. They are the ideal to what it means to be human.

To speak of an ideal component, therefore, is to speak about authenticity. Yet authenticity as an ideal is not a content per se; rather it is an ongoing activity of conversion, the fullness of self- transcendence. We saw earlier, however, how Adorno criticizes the use of this term *authenticity* because it lacks precision. According to Adorno, the use of this term results in a 'mixture of pseudo-objective concreteness and subjective idiosyncrasy. Without direct appeal to revelation or a spiritual authority ... the adepts of the jargon simulate the ascension of the word beyond the realm of the actual, conditioned, and contestable, giving the impression "as though a blessing from above were composed into that word.'"[70] For Lonergan, however, because authenticity is in actuality and activity, 'authenticity is realized when judgments of value are followed by decision and action, when knowing what is truly good leads to doing what truly is good.'[71] And doing what is truly good finds its proper fulfilment in an act of love that finds itself expressed in families and communities, and in the response to the divine ground's overwhelming love that floods our hearts. Moreover, 'once one has acted, made a decision, chosen a value one has not exhausted the content' of being authentic.[72] Being authentic is a continuous dialectic between development and decline. As Heidegger has shown us, 'time enters into the essence of being a man,' being authentic.[73] Neither Lonergan's nor Taylor's approach to the notion of authenticity falls prey to Adorno's criticism. Self-transcendence and authenticity go hand in hand, and authentic self-transcendence is conditioned by what we have named conversion. Analogous to the Platonic *periagoge*, which is the turning of the soul towards the Light, conversion in the fullest sense involves intellectual, moral, and religious transformations. Now while these three forms of conversion are distinct, they are 'three successive stages in a single achievement, the achievement of self-transcendence; and so attempts to separate and isolate the intellectual, the moral, and the religious are just so many efforts to distort or to entirely block authentic human development.'[74] While authenticity is not to be properly understood outside this threefold conversion, for the sake of clarity it will be helpful to address each type of conversion.[75] Thus, we begin with the issue of intellectual conversion.

Intellectual Conversion

Charles Taylor, in the preface to his latest collection of essays, lays out one of his principal themes and philosophical preoccupations that helps to bind the collection together – the issue of epistemology or what he calls 'the Hydra epistemology.'[76] Taylor is of the opinion that, beginning with Descartes, modern philosophy has focused its attention on the problem of knowledge and from there proceeded to delineate what one can 'legitimately say about other things: about God, or the world, or human life.'[77] The assumption behind this project is that we can possess clear knowledge about those things. To say something about God, the world, or human existence is to make knowledge claims. If we are to proceed this way, we need to first work out what knowledge is. For Taylor, this approach is a 'terrible and fateful illusion. It assumes wrongly that we can get to the bottom

of what knowledge is without drawing on our never-fully articulate understanding of human life and experience. There is a temptation here to a
kind of self-possessing clarity to which our modern culture has been almost
endlessly susceptible.'[78] Even those who think they have overcome Descartes have fallen into the problem of 'defining their ontology ... on the
basis of a prior doctrine of what we can know.'[79] In short, the 'pristine Cartesian ego has lost its autonomous purity through embodiment in nature
and embeddedness in history.'[80]

Given all this, then, what does it mean to say one is intellectually converted? According to Lonergan, intellectual conversion is brought about
by affirming one's self as a knower. In this moment of what Lonergan calls
self-affirmation, what is grasped is the dynamic finality of the conscious
subject. This dynamic finality is revealed through a primordial eros that
Lonergan calls the pure unrestricted desire to know. 'The desire to know
differs from other desires not just because it has a different object but
because it is a radically different kind of desire: under the sway of it reason
does not seek to possess, master, or control its object.'[81] We experience in
order to understand, we seek to understand in order to make judgments,
and we make judgments in order to know particular beings, and we want to
know particular beings so that we might know being in general. Intellectual conversion is the discovery of the erotic and transcendent nature of
human knowing. The importance of intellectual conversion is that it dis-
pels the notion that human knowing is a matter of taking a good look.
Intellectual conversion is necessary if we are to overcome the all too common myth that knowing is a mere matter of looking at something, knowing
in terms of 'ocular vision.'[82] In fact, Lonergan's critique of the epistemological tradition that knowing is some form of looking supports Richard
Rorty's belief that indeed the 'epistemological tradition has been held cap-
tive by ocular metaphors and argues that we must overcome the epistemological confusion that human knowledge is a re-presentation, or picture, of
what is out-there.'[83] However, where Rorty would have us adhere to a form
of anti-realism to avoid the inherent trap of epistemology, Lonergan
invites us to appropriate for ourselves the fact of critical realism as an alternative to the problem of knowing as some form of looking. Lonergan, like
Heidegger, 'opposes a 'forgetfullness of being' based on 'picture thinking.' Picture thinking does not acknowledge that 'the original relationship
of cognitional activity to the universe of being must lie in the intention of
being exercised in human questions for understanding and reflection.'[84]

In *Insight*, Lonergan gives us a phenomenological and hermeneutical
account of human intentionality, such that 'consciousness itself is not a
perception, but an experience, a usually tacit presence to ourselves that is
concomitant to our intentional and imaginally and linguistically mediated

presence to the world.'[85] Human knowing is not a single activity such as seeing, or understanding, or even judging. Rather, human knowing is a dynamic structure that is 'self-assembling, self-constituting. It puts itself together, one part summoning forth the next, till the whole is reached.'[86] It is the dynamic unity of consciousness as experiencing, understanding, and judging that constitutes human knowing in its fullest and truest sense. To have experienced, understood, and affirmed this dynamic unity is to be self-affirmed as a knower; self-affirmation posits the fact that the 'self as affirmed is characterized by such occurrences as sensing, perceiving, imagining, inquiring, understanding, formulating, reflecting, grasping, the unconditioned and affirming.'[87] And all of these operations flow out from 'the gift of the passionateness of being that underpins, accompanies, and reaches beyond the conscious subject.'[88] In short, intellectual conversion is the decision we make to accept the consequences of self-affirmation.

What is fundamental to intellectual conversion is that it pulls 'one out of the attitude that the world of sense is the criterion of reality.'[89] Again, intellectual conversion is crucial if we are ever to break the stranglehold of the counter-position that human knowing is associated with forms of looking. This myth about human knowing overlooks the important distinction between a world mediated by meaning and the world of immediacy. For Taylor, a world mediated by meaning means that 'we are in a sense surrounded by meaning; in the words we exchange, in all the signs we deploy, in the art, music, literature we create and enjoy, in the very shape of the man-made environment most of us live in.'[90] Lonergan understands this world mediated by meaning as follows:

> Again words express not merely what we have found out for ourselves but also all we care to learn from the memories of other men, from the common sense of the community, from the pages of literature, from the labors of scholars, from the investigations of scientists, from the experience of saints, from the meditations of philosophers and the theologians.[91]

Conversely, the world of immediacy is the sum of what is heard, touched, tasted, smelt, and felt. It is the world of the child before the acquisition of language, and it is the animal's world. And this is the problem. We develop first as animals before we develop as human beings. As a consequence, we confuse what is proper to human knowing with the type of knowing we share with animals.[92] This myth that knowing is a form of ocular vision sets up the dualism of the subject: it is the subject 'in here' trying to get out to the objects 'out there.' It is an epistemological confrontationism. 'The look as the basis of confrontationism may be sensitive perception as in the various forms of empiricism, or some intellectual intuitionism' as in Kantianism.[93] Again the source of this confrontationism is the myth that human knowing is really animal knowing. Thus we may be 'prone to make intelligence and reason merely another organ at the service of animal nature,'[94] which means that our orientation is merely towards successful living in the world of sense. While Taylor would not use the term *animal knowing*, still his analysis of the way in which human reason has become instrumentalized as merely a tool for determining means–ends relationships is in agreement with Lonergan's concerns.

Intellectual conversion is the affirmation of our self as a knower. To be self-affirmed this way means that we have grasped the dynamic unity and finality to the operations of human knowing. We grasp that the orientation of this dynamic structure is to a universe of being as manifested in the 'unfolding of a single thrust, the eros of the human spirit.'[95] We experience in order to understand, we seek to understand in order to judge, we judge in order to know particular beings, and we desire to know particular beings in order to know being in general. But being is not something that is known through some intuitive look. Being is known through the discursive raising and answering rational questions, and intellectual conversion is the explicit account of intentional self-transcendence. If we are truly converted intellectually then we have shifted our criterion of what is real from a mere private concern to a principle, which organizes ur world around the pure unrestricted desire to know. One who is intellectually converted realizes that knowing is essentially a dynamic process oriented to knowing being, 'to get beyond the subject, to reach what would be even if this subject happened not to exist.'[96] We never ask questions about 'nothing.' 'We should learn that questioning not only is about being but is being, being in its *Gelichtetheit* [luminousness], being in its openness to being, being that is realizing itself through inquiry to knowing that through knowing, it may come to loving.'[97] Taylor suggests this experience of the luminousness of being is a further elaboration of Heidegger's account of *Lichtung* (clearing). '*Lichtung* comes about through Being-in-the-world ... Coming to recognize this is part of a transformed stance toward the world in which the will to power is no longer central ... We are responding to something that is not us.'[98] As Lonergan puts the issue, 'Unconsciously operative is the finality that consists in the upwardly but indeterminately directed dynamism of all proportionate being. Consciously operative is the detached and disinterested desire raising ever further questions.'[99] In short, we desire to know the whole of being. And 'being as the objective of the pure desire to know includes the little bit that we already know and the vast expanse we could ask about.'[100] This notion of being 'is essentially dynamic, proleptic, an anticipation of the entirety, the concreteness, the totality that we ever intend and since our knowledge is finite never reach.'[101]

It has been affirmed that being is the object of all of our questioning. The intention of being, this eros of being, underpins all operations of human consciousness and all its contents. We clearly want to know what is true and real. However, while the intention of being is unrestricted, the realization of this intention is incremental. We can ask questions only one at a time. We come to know gradually and proportionally, given the nature of human understanding. Thus, our human judgments, as instances of the virtually unconditioned, 'possess that odd combination of normativity, fallibility and possible revisability.'[102] There is a great deal of humility that comes with being intellectually converted. We must confront our own contingency as knowers and realize that human knowing is not about power; rather, it is concerned with a radical self-honesty whereby we let the pure unrestricted desire to know unfold through the dynamic of the question in order to allow being to manifest itself, that is, to respond to something not in us. As a result, intellectual conversion is not only fundamental but also foundational if we are to move consistently out of the constant temptation, rooted in our biological patterning of human consciousness, to equate human knowing with various forms of animal knowing. If we are to properly develop, we must move from a world that is narrowly defined by our *Sorge* to a world defined by the pure desire to know and all the implications that brings.[103] To continue to equate what is true and real with our own concerns is to keep us from realizing the fullness of our nature as a knower. Our horizon remains excessively restricted and the possibility of development both personally and communally becomes increasingly problematic.

Intellectual conversion allows the intellect its full range of operations. The dynamic activity of questioning unfolds and brings us into a horizon of being, where the real is what is intelligible and not a subdivision of the already-out-there-now-real. Yet, concerning the question of living an authentic life, it is not enough to know what is true, what is real. Mere knowing does not constitute authentic human living. While it is true that authentic human existence demands intellectual conversion, still, mere knowing is not enough. To be truly reasonable demands 'consistency between what we know and what we do'; not only must there be a willingness to accept the truth of our intellectual conversion, we must also be willing to live up to that truth.[104] We must ask the further relevant question concerning the relationship between our knowing and our doing. Authentic human existence is always a question of a higher integration of what has gone before. This higher integration demands that what we know to be true, real, good, and valuable be translated into the choices we make and the actions we perform: 'knowing a world mediated by meaning is only a prelude to man's dealing with nature, to his interpersonal living and working with others, to his existential becoming what he is to make of himself by his own choices and deeds.'[105] There emerge, then, questions for deliberation and the issue of moral conversion.

Moral Conversion

The need for moral conversion is probably not readily apparent. Yet as Lonergan makes clear, the exigency for self-consistency in knowing and doing is revealed more in the ways we seek to mute this exigence. According to Lonergan, there are three elements involved in our efforts to avoid it. First, we seek to avoid self-knowledge, which means that we refuse to raise questions concerning who we are and why we do what we do. Second, there is the all too familiar act of rationalization. 'The average mind can invent lies about matters of fact; it can trump up excuses; it can allege extenuating circumstances that mingle fact with fiction.'[106] Third, there is the fall into despair. We seem more than willing to admit our failings, but there is no hope that we will be able to overcome them. In moral conversion, however, we courageously raise questions concerning our character; this in turn leads us to move out of the darkness of self-deception and seek the truth behind our actions, in order to ensure that there is harmony between what we claim to be and what in fact we are. Lastly, in spite of our own moral failings, which at times seem all too numerous, we have hope that our aspirations to moral wholeness are not so much whistling in the dark. In moral conversion, we seek to consistently opt for the truly worthwhile, the truly good, and the truly valuable rather than what appears to be merely good, valuable, or worthwhile. Moral conversion demands that our choice and subsequent decision be consonant with what one truly is, as opposed to the fulfilment of mere satisfaction. In moral self-transcendence 'we move beyond merely self-regarding norms and make ourselves as moral beings.'[107] Only in moral conversion can we hope to eclipse what Lonergan names the 'three-fold escape of fleeing self-consciousness.' To speak about moral conversion, therefore, necessitates that we speak about our understanding of what it is that we are choosing in each and every situation. This involves an articulation of transcendental value, or what Taylor would call a hypergood.

Just as the intelligible is what is intended in questions for intelligence, and truth and being in questions for reflection, it is value that is intended in questions for deliberations. 'It is by appealing to value or values that we satisfy some appetites and do not satisfy others, that we approve some systems for achieving the good of order and disapprove of others, that we praise or blame human persons as good or evil and their actions as right or wrong.'[108] It is questions for deliberation, then, that seek to determine the worthwhileness of a given course of action, or the goodness of a particular object. 'In general, response to value both carries us towards self transcendence and selects an object for the sake of whom or of which we transcend ourselves.'[109]

In our chapter on Taylor we saw that the question of the good, and therefore what it means for us to be authentic, could not be disassociated from the human power to evaluate one's desires. According to Taylor, our affective life manifests for us 'a sense of what is important to us qua subject, or to put it slightly differently, of what we value, or what matters to us, in the life of the subject.'[110] Feelings reflect not only our moral situation but also the situation as it truly is.[111] That is, feelings reveal to us the significance of a given situation. 'We are picking out what in the situation gives the grounds or basis for our feelings or what should give such grounds.'[112] It is our feelings, then, such as shame, remorse, pride, or joy that reveal to us what we value most. Lonergan, as Taylor, understands feelings as intentional response to values. It is through feelings that the values that we deliberate upon are revealed. Through feelings we are placed in relationship to objects. Feelings then give 'intentional consciousness its mass, momentum, drive, power. Without these feelings our knowing and deciding would be paper thin.'[113]

> Because of our feelings, our desires and our fears, our hope or
> despair, our joys and sorrow, our enthusiasm and indignation, our
> esteem and contempt, our trust and distrust, our love and hatred, our
> tenderness and wrath, our admiration, veneration, reverence, our
> dread, horror, terror, we are oriented massively and dynamically in a
> world mediated by meaning.[114]

For Lonergan, feelings regard two classes of objects. First, there are those that one finds pleasant or unpleasant, agreeable or not agreeable. Second, there are objects of value. These include what Lonergan calls the ontic value of persons, and the qualitative values that one finds in beauty, truth, and a life of virtue. Moreover, these values are subject to a hierarchy of preference. One moves from the vital group of values, such as health (physical and mental), to social values, such as 'family, custom, society, education, state, law, economy, technology, church.'[115] These are followed by cultural values such as art, religion, philosophy, history, language, literature, science, and theology.

Last, there is personal value. For Lonergan, this is the person in her selftranscendence. It is the person loving, and being loved, caring, and being cared for. Each time the person decides for what is truly worthwhile, what is truly good versus what is apparently good, she continues to constitute herself as morally converted and hence self-transcendent. Moral conversion means the person has committed herself to move beyond feelings that are merely ego-regarding, in order to live in a world where she constitutes herself as an original value, and as someone who originates values, which in turn bring about values that are terminal.[116] Terminal values are chosen instances of what are indeed good, worthwhile, which also include the truthfulness of a particular good of order. In the choice of terminal values the person is involved in the dialectical process of progress or decline. The person as originating value is the one who is doing the choosing; she is an authentic person achieving self-transcendence through her good choices.[117]

We have seen that the person who is morally converted is not only an originator of value, but he is also a person who is making judgments of value. These judgments of value may be either simple or comparative. Simple judgments of value posit that this something is truly good, valuable, or worthwhile; on the other hand, comparative judgments, as the name implies, state that something is better than something else, or one course of action is more appropriate than another.[118] These types of value judgments may be objective or subjective. Objective judgments of value are judgments made by the person as morally self-transcendent. Merely subjective value judgments are only ego-regarding. The truth or falsity of one's value judgment resides in the conversion or lack of conversion of the person making the choice. In other words, 'judgments of fact purport to state what is or is not so; judgments of value state or purport to state what is or is not truly good or really better.'[119] 'Judgments of value will be responsible only in so far as they are motivated by an act of reflective understanding which grasps the possible course of action as virtually unconditioned value. Judgments of value provide but an initial thrust towards moral self-transcendence.'[120] Complete moral self-transcendence terminates in decision and the acts that follow upon those decisions.

Just as the fulfilling conditions for a judgment of fact are to be found within the intellectual subject, the fulfilling conditions for judgments of value are to be found within the existential subject. 'Their truth or falsity, accordingly has its criterion in the authenticity or the lack of authenticity of the subject's being.'[121] The existential subject is fundamentally aware that in each and every situation what is at stake is not only one's identity, but one's destiny as well.[122] It is through judgments of value and the subsequent decisions and actions that one not only commits oneself to a particular course of action, but constitutes oneself as a moral being – a being capable of truly loving, and shaping not only one's own destiny but the broader world in which one lives. It must be emphasized that it 'is in acts of deciding, and only in acts of deciding that values are actualized.'[123] In addition, decisions actualize two things: 'a reality independent of oneself realized thorough one's course of action, and the being one becomes through such a course of action.'[124] Thus, it is by judgments of value and the decisions to actualize those values that one makes oneself either an authentic person performing consistent acts of self-transcendence, or an inauthentic person who is mired in the abyss of his or her own egoism.

Moral conversion is a profound awareness that by one's decision one makes not only oneself and one's world but also the world that others will inherit. Moral conversion is the inner transformation of the person that flows out to effect an outer transformation of the world. Finally, one commits oneself to a moral way of life because it is 'existentially' grasped as the valuable thing to do. One comes to the insight that 'moral self-transcendence opens up a new horizon of possibility – the possibility of benevolence and beneficence, of honest collaboration and of true love, of swinging completely out of the habitat of an animal and of becoming a person in a human society.'[125]

Religious Conversion

What is it, though, that effects moral conversion? It is one thing to know what we should do; it is quite another to actually choose to do what is truly worthwhile, valuable, or good. While we possesses the capacity for moral self-transcendence, it remains only a possibility until we fall in love, because 'then one's being becomes being-in-love ... It is the first principle. From it flow one's desires and fears, one's joys and sorrows, one's discernment of values, one's decisions and deeds.'[126] Being-in-love brings us to a new level of understanding of values. What begins to unfold is that decisions and choices about what is worthwhile no longer pivot upon ego-regarding norms. Rather, being-in-love is now a concern for the other. Being-in-love is essentially dynamic. 'It is about an energy that smashes through the surface of everyday awareness and makes possible an exchange of spiritual power and knowledge which not only penetrates the lovers through every aspect of body, mind and spirit, but reaches far beyond them to transform other relationships and the very aspect of the material world.'[127]

As Bernard Lonergan puts the issue, when we fall in love 'then life begins anew. A new principle takes over and, as long as it lasts, we are lifted above our selves and carried along as parts within an ever more intimate yet ever more liberating dynamic whole.'[128] For Lonergan this being-in-love is of different kinds. There is the intimate love between husband and wife, love of children, love of one's country, and love for our neighbour. Each of these forms of love manifests itself in the care, concern, and welfare that is exhibited towards the object of love. Our world undergoes a new and vital reorganization. There is another form of love, however, from which all other forms of love are derived. It is 'unrestricted being-in-love.' Just as the basic experience of being-in-love reveals values hitherto unnoticed, so also being in love with the divine ground is the fulfilment of moral conversion that brings 'deep joy and profound peace. Our love reveals to us values we had not appreciated, values of prayer and worship, or repentance and belief.'[129] Being in love with the divine ground reveals to us to whom we are ultimately responsible and to whom we ultimately respond in self-transcending love.[130]

For Lonergan, just as 'the question of God is implicit in all our questioning, so being in love with God is the basic fulfillment of our conscious intentionality.'[131] To be truly in love with God is to be religiously converted. It is God's prior and ongoing love for each one of us that makes possible our being in love with God. To be religiously converted means that our love of God is without conditions, qualifications, or reservations.[132] Just as unrestricted questioning is our capacity for self-transcendence, so being in love in an unrestricted fashion is the proper fulflment of that capacity. Religious conversion takes into itself, or sublates (to use Lonergan's term) both intellectual and moral conversion. Just as absolute being is what is intended in our questioning, and absolute goodness in acts of deliberation, so being-in-love in an unrestricted fashion, that is, falling completely in love with God, 'is the fulfilment of my unrestricted thrust to self-transcendence through intelligence and truth and responsibility, because the one that fulfils that thrust must be supreme in intelligence, truth, goodness.'[133] Thus, being in love with God is not a matter of our knowing or choosing. It is God's grasp of us in the depth of our being, where our horizons of knowing and doing are abolished, dismantled, and reorganized within a new horizon 'in which the love of God will transvalue our values and the eyes of that love will transform our knowing.'[134] Being in love with God brings to perfection the totality of our conscious operations.[135] It is the love of God that is now the ultimate ground and source for all of our intentional activity. This type of love manifests itself in an ongoing experience of joy and peace, and these in turn are manifested in acts of 'kindness, goodness, fidelity, gentleness, and self-control.'[136] The effects of religious conversion bring about a fulfilment, a wholeness to one's being. The wholeness that comes with being in love with God in an unrestricted fashion manifests itself in love and concern for the other as beloved. Religious conversion may be understood as the 'basic and radical displacement of the subject ... Then the epitome of responsibility for the other is achieved when we fall in love with the mystery of love and awe.'[137] Without religious conversion, the originating value is not God but the person, and the terminal value is alone the human good. Through the eyes of religious love, however, 'the originating value is divine light and love, while terminal value is the whole universe.'[138]

Lastly, to say that one is conscious of this state is not to say that it is known. Knowing in the true sense is the compound set of operations of experiencing, understanding, and judging. None of these operations by itself is knowing in the strict sense. As long as this conscious and dynamic state of being in love in an unrestricted fashion remains unthematized, it is an experience of mystery. But because this mystery is tied to being in love it is overpowering and fascinating:

> To it one belongs; by it one is possessed. Because it is an unmeasured love, the mystery evokes awe. Of itself, then, inasmuch as it is conscious without being known, the gift of God's love is an experience of the holy, of Rudolf Otto's *mysterium fascinans et tremendum*. It is what Paul Tillich named a being grasped by ultimate concern. It corresponds to St Ignatius Loyola's consolation that has no cause.[139]

The fulfilment that is God's love is the completion and fulfilment of the person. Falling in love with God is the fulfilment of what it means to be an authentic human being, and this fulfilment overflows into love of one's neighbour as oneself. In short, being in love with God is a collaboration and cooperation with God and others to sustain and realize the order of the universe.[140]

Perhaps the reader, even now, is still asking, what is authenticity for Lonergan? To summarize, the person achieves authenticity in self-transcendence. Self-transcendence is achieved in intellectual, moral, and religious conversion. Thus the authentic person struggles with the ongoing exigencies of conversion, which are expressed by the transcendental imperatives: be attentive, be intelligent, be reasonable, and be responsible. Without intellectual conversion the person will consistently mistake the world of sense for the world mediated by meaning; without moral conversion, what is truly worthwhile and good will be understood in terms of values as ego-regarding, and without religious conversion one is 'radically desolate: in a world without hope and without God.'[141]

Still why speak of authenticity in terms of conversion? Why not suggest that it is a matter of choosing some practical ideal and leave the discussion at determining what ideal is to be chosen? The difficulty with that position seems to place one into a counter-position of decisionism, whereby it is merely my choice that confers authenticity and goodness. Again, such a suggestion does not squarely face the question of human development and our inability to sustain this development. In other words, mere deciding cannot solve the problem of what Lonergan calls the 'surd.' 'Decisions are wrong, not because of their private or public origin, but because they diverge from the dictates of intelligence and reasonableness.'[142] In the long run, it is the problem of bias, whether dramatic, individual, group, or general that militates against any notion of authenticity in terms of choosing an ideal. As Lonergan is quick to point out, the surd does not reside in outer things, but in the minds and hearts of human beings.[143] As a result, 'each successive batch of possible and practical courses of action is screened to eliminate as unpractical whatever does not seem practical to an intelligence and a willingness that not only are developed imperfectly but also suffer from bias. But the social situation is the cumulative product of individual and group decisions, and as these decisions depart from the demands of intelligence and reasonableness, so the social situation becomes like the complex number, a compound of the rational and irrational.'[144] The problem is further exacerbated by the fact that this distorted social situation provides the ongoing material for choices and decisions. If indeed authenticity were a matter of choosing an ideal, then it seems that the ideal itself is already shaped by this distorted social situation. So the problem of human development is not just a matter of choosing the right ideal, for the ideal is most likely already clouded by a conflict between positions and counter-positions. No, the solution has to be a higher integration to human living. Perhaps it would be helpful to quote Lonergan at length:

> The solution has to be a still higher integration of human living. For the problem is radical and permanent ... it is not met by revolutionary change, nor by human discovery, nor by the enforced implementation of discovery; it is as large as human living and human history. Further, the solution has to take people just as they are. If it is to be a solution and not a mere suppression of the problem, it has to acknowledge and respect and work through man's intelligence and reasonableness and freedom. It may eliminate neither development nor tension yet it must be able to replace incapacity by capacity for sustained development. Only a still higher integration can meet such requirements. For only a higher integration leaves underlying manifolds with the autonomy yet succeeds in introducing a higher systematization into their nonsystematic coincidences.[145]

It is only in a conversion that is intellectual, moral, and religious that a higher integration of human living is made possible; only in conversion does the person confront his or her inability to sustain personal and communal development. It is this threefold conversion that opens the subject up most fully as a human being. We may say, then, that human authenticity is the law of integration. The exigency of Dasein is to wholeness and completion, and this exigency to wholeness is towards more than just the whole human good. Martha Nussbaum, by way of contrast, splits the question of self-transcendence, and hence the nature of the good, into internal as opposed to external. Internal self-transcendence is a pushing for human excellence 'against the limits that constrain human life.'[146] Internal transcendence concerns itself with the human condition in that we 'want [ourselves] and others not to be hungry, not to be ill, not to be without shelter, not to be betrayed or bereaved, not to lose any of one's faculties – and to strive as hard as one possibly can to bring all that about in life.'[147] Conversely, in her view external transcendence seems to be associated with the afterlife and God's existence in the Judaeo-Christian context. This type of transcendence 'seems to undercut the motivation to push hard in this direction [human excellence]. If one thinks that the really important thing is to get over to a different sort of life altogether, then this may well make one work less hard on this one.'[148]

Taylor, at the end of *Sources of the Self*, is also sensitive to what may be described as Nussbaum's 'neo-Lucretian' outlook. Although our 'highest spiritual ideals and aspirations also threaten to lay the most crushing burdens on humankind,'[149] the various naturalist and Nietzschean critiques of self-sacrifice make 'the cardinal mistake of believing that a good must be invalid if it leads to suffering or destruction.'[150] Moreover, adopting what Taylor calls a stripped-down secular outlook absent of any religious hope for the future is itself a form of mutilation.[151] In short, Taylor sees a large element of hope in the Judaeo-Christian tradition in spite of the actions of some of its believers. This hope is grounded in its 'central promise of a divine affirmation of the human, more total than humans can ever attain unaided.'[152] Similarly for Lonergan, the fullness of human integration takes place only when one falls in love with God in an unrestricted manner. One's whole world is changed and reoriented around the mystery of absolute love. In addition, given the dynamic orientation and structure to human consciousness, self-transcendence is of a piece.[153] The whole human good is taken with absolute seriousness, because at its root is a desire for that goodness beyond all good. It is only in religious conversion that the issue of the whole human good can be adequately addressed. Being in love with God solves the threefold problem of flight from self-understanding, rationalization, and moral despair. To love God with one's whole heart, mind, and soul is to live in joy; it is to be rigorously honest about who I am and why I do the things that I do. Lastly, love of God fills us with a hope that the 'power of God's love brings forth a new energy and efficacy in all goodness, and the limit of human expectation ceases to be the grave.'[154] Instead of opting for Mark Anthony's position in which the good that we do is buried with us, while the evil seems to live on, authenticity 'recognizes that God grants men their freedom, that he wills them to be persons and not just automata, that he calls them to the higher authenticity that overcomes evil with good.'[155] Human progress and authenticity are linked together. Only in authenticity can one hope to meet the challenge of progress and decline. Or perhaps the simple and compact words of Julian of Norwich sum up what authenticity truly means: 'Truth sees God, wisdom perceives God, and from these two comes a third – holy wondering delight in God, which is love. Where there is truth and wisdom, there is also true love, springing from them both. And it is all of God's making.'[156]

In summary, Lonergan's account of intellectual, moral, and religious self-transcendence gives meaning to each of the many levels of human reality, and so also meaning to the whole. Attentiveness, intelligence, reasonableness, responsibility, and loving are, in a phrase Lonergan borrows from Gerard Manley Hopkins, different 'self-tastes,' yet together they form a single stream.[157] Realizing concretely the meaning of the whole means falling in love. 'So the experience of being-in-love is an experience of fulfilment, of complete integration, of a self-actualization that is an unbounded source of good will and good deeds.'[158]

4

Taylor and Lonergan: Dialogue and Dialectic

With the drawing of this Love and the voice of this Calling
We shall not cease from exploration
And the end of all our exploring
Will be to arrive where we started
And know the place for the first time.

– T.S. Eliot, 'Little Gidding'

The common thread that has bound the previous chapters together is the question of what it means to be an authentic person. We have seen that for Heidegger human authenticity is bound to the appropriation of one's death and one's own historicity. But, in the end, Heidegger's position closes off the possibility of transcendence and leaves death as the only horizon. Taylor spoke of authenticity as a transcendent moral ideal whereby one acts as one ought and not merely as one wants. Bernard Lonergan specifically spoke of authenticity as self-transcendence. And authentic self-transcendence entails a threefold conversion that is intellectual, moral, and religious. Still, the reader may be asking what really is so important about the meaning of authenticity. To begin with, this question of authenticity seems even more urgent now. 'As individuals become more and more deeply entangled in a rapidly changing and ever more diverse world, the business of soul-making appears to be at once more pressing and less certain than in earlier eras. Change becomes an abiding feature of experience and raises doubts about obscure guideposts that previously had directed journeying pilgrims.'[1] Moreover, the desire 'to be authentic' is common currency in any discussion that remotely addresses the Ancients' question about the best way to live, so it is important to articulate exactly what we mean by being authentic, and that importance pivots upon the issues of human progress and decline. Both Lonergan and Taylor are aware that a society's understanding of what it means to be authentically human shapes its institutions.[2] Hence, clarifying what authenticity means in terms of human living regards our common destiny as men and women. Getting it right has enormous consequences for our future. In short, both Taylor and Lonergan are seeking a 'Socratic reversal.' This 'entails a radical displacement of any person's average "self-image" from the self to what is highest and best. This calls for a revolution in our living, and usually, a new solution to the problem of living together.'[3]

Lonergan and Taylor have shown that human existence and human understanding are a historically dynamic and complex relationship between the person and culture. Both stress the historicity of the human subject, and both dismantle Cartesian certitude and the Kantian transcendental ego. Lonergan and Taylor have de-centred the subject by showing to what degree our self-understanding is conditioned from above downwards by the facticity of human existence.[4] Both have articulated, in response to postmodernism's critique of what Heidegger called 'humanism,' how indeed the person is not truncated, neglected, or immanentist, but existential, and each has done so from a particular but complementary viewpoint.

Lonergan uses a spatial metaphor of the way up and the way down to show how the person is both a constituting and constituted subject.[5] The way down describes the lived and already given cultural and linguistic matrix (which is historical) that structures the person's sense of identity. The way up explains the constituting activity of the human subject: the intentional activity of the person as she constitutes herself to be a knower, chooser, and lover.

Taylor, with his genealogical account of the modern self, has given a rich analysis of the 'way down,' of how we currently understand ourselves as being-in-the-world. Conversely, Lonergan with his cognitional theory has provided a more differentiated account of the way up. In short, Lonergan rearticulated the 'hermeneutical circle in terms of the two vectors of human development: the way of achievement from below upwards, and the way of gift or heritage from above downwards.'[6] This hermeneutic circle is the context for raising and answering this question of what it means to be authentically human. It serves as the source, or sources, out of which our understanding of human authenticity will arise. While Taylor has given us a richer description of this 'way of gift or heritage,' Lonergan provides us with what I take to be a more differentiated account of the normative nature of the engaged agent. This is not to say that Taylor eschews such a notion. After all, Taylor consistently emphasizes the normativity to our nature as linguistic beings, the linguistic intentionality that is operative in us as dialogical beings. Where Taylor seems more comfortable with articulating 'the human experience of truth as hermeneutic, by tacitly highlighting the role of questioning and the *phronesis* character of judgment ... [Lonergan] is clearer about rejecting the positivist or Kantian conception of knowledge as a combination of concepts and empirical intuitions within the horizon of *Vorhan-denheit*.'[7] In short, I will suggest that it is Lonergan's account of cognitional theory (what am I doing when I am knowing) and the self-appropriation that it entails, that has the capacity to move the conversation of what it means to be an authentic human being beyond what Taylor calls the 'liberalism of neutrality.' Cognitional theory can provide a richer and more differentiated account of what Taylor (and by extension Heidegger) has tried to articulate in terms of Dasein as being-in-the-world, and Dasein's exigency for being-a-whole-self: 'the truth of human existence.'

We have seen that Taylor and Lonergan think that human authenticity – the truth of human existence – involves the experience of conversion. In Taylor, this experience is nascently moral and religious. For Lonergan it is explicitly named intellectual, moral, and religious conversion. This last chapter, then, will sharpen the similarities and differences between Taylor and Lonergan on the relationship of conversion to authenticity, by focusing on three fundamental and interconnected sources within the hermeneutic circle: art, cognitional theory, and the human good. It is these three elements that most closely bind these thinkers together, as well as manifest their fundamental differences. This will be followed by an excursus suggesting that the importance of Lonergan's notion of authenticity is to be found in a more differentiated understanding of the converted subject than we get with Taylor. Thus, this chapter will be divided into four individual sections, each with its own subheadings.

Art

Within the context of engaged agency, Taylor draws upon the idea of a framing epiphany as one of these sources outside the self, but not in the Cartesian sense of the subject in here over against the object out there. Rather, 'when technology has become the ontology of the world, the oblivion of being demands a massive reversal of human orientation towards a poetic dwelling that attends to the *Fragwürdigkeit des Seins*.'[8]

For Taylor, human existence is a quest for meaning and significance. Not to have a framework for this quest is to 'fall into a life which is spiritually senseless.'[9] Taylor's concern then, is to find 'moral sources *outside* the subject through languages that resonate within him or her, the grasping of an order which is inseparably indexed to a personal vision.'[10] The notion of epiphany identifies those independent sources, which serve as the locus for one's authentic ideal. Epiphanies manifest that which is other. They issue from the call of the 'world' understood as an independent matrix of meaning from which one's idea of what it means to be authentic is revealed. An epiphany discloses something beyond us that makes demands upon us, or calls us. It is in modern art and poetry that we find the clearest expression of epiphanic events. Modern art and poetry seem to respect modernity's concern for the subject, without falling into an aberrant subjectivism. Modern art is an once inward, yet it involves the de-centring of the subject.[11] The central issue of epiphany, for which Rilke is the quintessential example, is 'not just our action, but it involves a transaction between ourselves and the world.'[12] For Taylor, epiphany works against the idea that the telos of human existence is merely an inwardly generated activity tied to nothing beyond itself. An epiphany frees us from the debased mechanistic world, and it brings 'to light the spiritual reality behind natural and uncorrupted human feelings.'[13] An epiphanic event functions as a source of authenticity because it enables one to see the good, and thereby empowers us to orient our life in terms of this ideal.[14] In other words, epiphanic art completes us 'through expressions which reveal and define'[15] what it means for us to be authentic.

   'Since the era of the great chain of being and the publicly established order of references,' nothing in 'the domain of mythology, metaphysics, or theology stands in this fashion as publicly available background today.'[16] A publicly established order of reference may be understood as sets of beliefs and practices that are part of the 'tacit background of objects of reliance, of things that are ready-to-hand in Heidegger's language.'[17] Nonetheless, epiphanic art at some level encompasses some commonly held belief positions, but its stance towards these positions is much more tentative than in the old public creeds.[18] 'It is also that what I call their personal index makes them a different kind of thing. We know that the poet, if he is serious, is pointing to something – God, the tradition – which he believes to be there for all of us. But we also know that he can only give it to us refracted through his own sensibility. We cannot just detach the nugget of transcendent truth; it is inseparably imbedded in the work.'[19] In the following poetic excerpt from Wallace Stevens, we find what Taylor sees as one of the clearest examples of the melding of the transcendent and the subjective.

   The world about us would be desolate except for the world within us. The major poetic idea in the world is and always has been the idea of God.

After one has abandoned a belief in God, poetry is the essence which takes its place as life's redemption.[20]

We now live in an age where a common order of public meaning is no longer accessible. 'But that doesn't mean there is nothing in those domains (theology, metaphysics, morality) that poets may not want to reach out to in order to say what they want to say.'[21] What it does mean is by opening up these horizons the poet/artist articulates a personal vision. The only way, then, we can understand the order in which we find ourselves is through a 'personal resonance' with what the artist is expressing. For instance, reading someone like Rilke places us in a situation in which our desire for self-realization stands in relationship to something outside ourselves calling to us, making demands upon us. Each of us has an aspiration to wholeness that is possible only to the degree that we commit ourselves to something beyond our own desires. Epiphanic art discloses to us how self-determining freedom and our desire to be authentic depends on something noble, courageous, or holy, that calls to us independent of our will. True freedom, therefore, means choosing between alternatives that either move us to a greater realization of our ideal of authenticity, or imprison us in a world that perpetuates a life of baseness or cowardice.

Taylor's account of the experience of epiphanic art is analogous to Lonergan's account of the aesthetic patterning of consciousness. For the person, living is more than mere concern for vital living; one does not live by bread alone, or so the saying goes. 'Conscious living is itself a joy that reveals its spontaneous authenticity in the various forms of play that moves through childhood, adolescence then into adult living.'[22] As an adult, this joy is manifested as one allows oneself to be swept away by Gorecki's *Third Symphony*, or to be gathered up into Chagall's *Crossing of the Red Sea*. Such are instances of a distinct pattern that not only affords us the opportunity for a richer and deeper form of living beyond the merely biological, but it also offers the possibility of a twofold freedom. First, it can free us from merely biological concerns of human living by transporting us to a world of adventure, greatness, majesty, and goodness.[23] Second, it can free us from a tyrannical form of common sense that judges solely in terms of usefulness,[24] or a stultifying form of intelligence that is constrained by mathematical proofs and the need for scientific verification.[25] Because of this freedom, the work of art is allowed to be itself. It is in and through the artistic media that the artist expresses his or her insights into human living. 'It seeks to mean, to convey, to impart something that is to be reached, not through science or philosophy, but through a participation and, in some fashion, a reenactment of the artist's inspiration and intention.'[26]

For Lonergan, art is to be understood as 'the objectification of a purely experiential pattern.'[27] Art as an objectification of a pattern implies that there exists within the work itself intrinsic relationships among colours, tones, movements, and so forth. The objectification of the pattern expresses what has been perceived by the artist, as well as 'a pattern of the feelings that flow out of and are connected with the perceiving.'[28] The pattern is pure because the experiencing that it orders is given its full range. It is not circumscribed by a particular type of orientation, whether intellectual or ideological. It is the heard as heard, the felt as felt, the seen as seen; nothing foreign or extraneous to the perceiving has been introduced into consciousness. The pattern as pure lets experience 'find its full complement of feeling. It lets experiencing fall into its own proper patterns ... So experiencing becomes rhythmic, one movement necessitating another and the other in turn necessitating the first. Tensions are built up to be resolved.'[29] This pure pattern is then objectified in the work of art itself. As objectification of this pure pattern, the work of art expresses what the artist has intentionally grasped as most significant, of utmost concern and value in the pure pattern of experiencing.

Art, as the objectification of a purely experiential pattern, is symbolic. Like Taylor, Lonergan also understands art as epiphanic. Art draws 'attention to the fact that the splendor of the world is a cipher, a revelation, an unveiling; it is the presence of one who is not seen, touched, grasped, put in a genus, distinguished by difference yet is present.'[30] The symbolic nature of art, then, is an invitation to immerse oneself in this revelatory event, to be released from the day-to-day routine of common-sense living, and in that release discover new and richer possibilities for authentic human living. Art is elemental in its meaning, but profound in its implications for the whole intentional orientation of a subject and his or her community. Art is an expression of wonder in its most elemental and grandest sweep.[31]

The human capacity for art not only breaks the bonds of biological determinism, but it also expresses what Lonergan calls a 'flexibility that makes it a ready tool for the spirit of inquiry.'[32] To say that art is a ready tool for the spirit of inquiry is to merely state the obvious: art can elicit wonder, which in turn raises questions regarding what it is the artist is trying to articulate, through images, colours, sounds, and words, what is most worthwhile.

The importance here between Taylor and Lonergan is that while Taylor's account of the expressivist turn in modernity is more substantial, each thinker, however, has grasped the significance of art as a constitutive element within the hermeneutic circle. In other words, both thinkers understand the power of art to set the conditions for the experience of self-transcendence both morally and spiritually.

Cognitional Theory

We know from Lonergan's phenomenological analysis of human consciousness that it is a dynamically related self-assembling pattern. It is self-
assembling because each level of operations is summoned forth by the
next until the whole is reached. In its broad lines this 'dynamism rests on
operators that promote activity from one level to the next. The operators
are a priori, and they alone are a priori. Their content is ever an anticipation of the next level of operations and thereby is not to be found in the
contents of the previous level.'[33] As explained in chapter 2, the operators
are questions for intelligence, reflection, and deliberation. Building on the
level of experience, these operators yield the four levels of conscious operation. Moreover, the lower level prepares for or conditions the higher and
then is sublated by it.[34] To use Lonergan's own words to sum up this notion
of consciousness as a dynamic operation,

> We experience to have the materials for understanding; and under-
> standing, so far from cramping experience, organizes it, enlarges its
> range, refines its content, and directs it to a higher goal. We under-
> stand and formulate to be able to judge, but judgment calls for ever
> fuller experience and better understanding; and that demand has us
> clarifying and expanding and applying our distinctions between
> astronomy and astrology, chemistry and alchemy, history and legend,
> philosophy and myth, fact and fiction. We experience and under-
> stand and judge to become moral: to become moral practically, for
> our decisions affect other things; to become moral interpersonally,
> for our decisions affect other persons; to become moral existentially,
> for by our decisions we constitute what we are to be.[35]

In contrast, Taylor's account of self-transcendence is focused more upon a
hermeneutics of judgments: 'We experience our world as worded: Our
world is always a foreground for us through interpretations.'[36] Taylor wants
to clarify the conditions of intentionality by showing that even 'in our theoretical stance to the world, we are agents ... coping with things ... Once we
take this point, then the entire epistemological position is undermined.
Obviously foundationalism goes, since our representations of things – the
kind of objects we pick out as a whole, enduring entities – are grounded in
the way we deal with those things.'[37] Taylor understands intentional consciousness as an existential hermeneutics of objects, a horizon analysis in
which consciousness is perception or awareness of something. 'Our perception of the world is essentially that of an embodied agent, engaged with

or at grips with the world.'[38] In short, 'consciousness as perception objectifies what it is aware of.'[39] For Lonergan, perception (through which our experience of something comes already patterned in a particular way) mediates 'to us neither appearance nor reality, but data,' and these data must be clarified through further questions.[40] Of course Taylor would not disagree with the point about the need for questioning what we have perceived. Reason is the ability 'to articulate the background of our lives perspicuously.'[41] Where Taylor focuses on the hermeneutics of objects and their framing horizon of meaning, Lonergan maintains that a fuller account of self-transcendence involves a further hermeneutical and phenomenological account of the conscious operations of the person that terminate in 'deliberation, decision, and action.'[42]

> Again, when we analyze operations as conscious we begin with conscious operations as intentional (perceiving, wondering about, understanding, criticizing this or that object) ... But this is only part of what is involved in our asking and answering questions as we come to know. As our explicit awareness of both the subject-pole and object-pole of our conscious intending expands, it will inevitably lead to our realizing the historical conditionedness of our conscious acts. Thus we become increasingly aware of the formative influence upon us of emotions, of the way we are peculiarly conditioned by our intellectual, social, cultural, aesthetic, moral and spiritual development. In brief intentionality analysis naturally expands into horizon analysis.[43]

We may say that Lonergan brings Taylor's hermeneutical enterprise to its full conclusion by articulating what Fred Lawrence has termed Lonergan's 'hermeneutics of interiority as cognitive, and his hermeneutics of interiority as existential.' Put another way, Lonergan begins with the 'polymorphous existential [not existentialist] subject, and by generalized empirical method lays bare the immanent and operative dynamism of conscious intentionality ... He goes beyond the horizons of the truncated, immanentist, and alienated subjects to disclose a total viewpoint that, precisely because it gets beyond those other foreshortened or distorted horizons, is basic yet not foundationalist.'[44]

It would be appropriate at this juncture to address, once again, the questionable assumption that Lonergan's hermeneutical analysis of our cognitional operations is really just another form of foundationalism. One of Taylor's major criticisms of modern epistemology is that clarity and validity are the criteria for knowing anything as true, and these are possible only to the degree that we follow a set of rules, a reliable method that can generate 'well-founded-confidence' and certainty.[45] This saddles us with a Cartesian formalism, and a foundationalism whereby the method of natural science and sense data alone are the criteria for what is real.

Lonergan is just as worried as Taylor about dead ends in epistemology. But when Lonergan speaks of method, particularly the general empirical method, it is not to be confused with the kind of method Taylor equates with Cartesian or Kantian accounts of the mind's operations. Lonergan's method is indeed empirical because one is appealing to the experience of sense data, but also to the experience of one's own conscious operations: experiencing, understanding, judging, deciding, and loving. This appeal has been directed not primarily to objects but to 'the operations through which subjects and objects are mediated cognitionally, morally and religiously.'[46] Unlike Descartes who objectified consciousness as some inner look, 'Lonergan's notion of consciousness is prior to and distinct from any later process in which we heighten our awareness through inquiring about and understanding through checking out and judging what we undergo.'[47] Lonergan understands knowledge as performative – it is knowledge of the subject as subject in act (engaged) and not as an object.[48] While we speak of cognitional operations as experiencing, understanding, judging, deciding, and loving, this is not to suggest some simple recipe one follows to its logical and clear conclusion. All of these operations are conditioned by prior operations and fraught with contingency. There are biases, scotomas, not to mention the fact that the 'intentional subject is radically polymorphic rather than uniform. The desire to know competes with numerous other desires for the attention and allegiance of the subject.'[49] One can indeed speak of Lonergan's general empirical method as basic and simultaneously acknowledge that acts of human knowing are shot through with contingency, For example, how intelligent have I been, how reasonable have I been, how attentive, etc.? There is the 'sheer historicity [and facticity] of the lower manifolds of the sensing subject. Some people just see or hear less well than others.'[50] Lonergan, unlike Foucault, does not proclaim the death of the subject. But he does take the postmodern turn by overcoming the Kantian and Cartesian subject by showing that true self-transcendence is manifested in act. Lonergan, like Heidegger, 'insists that as intelligent, reasonable, and responsible, we finite human beings use language to get beyond ourselves in knowing reality and in transforming it.'[51]

Both Lonergan and Taylor understand that one's identity is constituted by a horizon, the person's being-in-the-world. 'The broadening, deepening, developing of the horizon, world, blik is also the broadening, deepening, developing of the subject, the self, the ego. The development that is the constitution of one's world is also the constitution of one's self.'[52] One's self-understanding, one's identity is never separated from one's world. To understand myself I must understand *my* world, and this understanding is never exhausted, nor is it ever a thing to be possessed in some final way. For the very eros of being, if not diverted by other desires such as power, consistently calls the subject to a deeper and deeper level of involved self-understanding as cognitional and as existential.

Knowing from Above Downwards

This crucial development of one's identity and one's world begins within a cultural context that has a history. Both thinkers show how we find ourselves already immersed within a particular heritage, and our self-understanding is never outside of this context. It is this notion of a heritage that accounts for what Lonergan and Taylor consider knowledge from above downwards. More precisely, the issue of a heritage is concerned with the role that belief plays in Lonergan's hermeneutics of cognition and Taylor's linguistic intentionality.

Together, Lonergan and Taylor are clear that our coming to know is a common enterprise. It is a collaboration of ourselves with others in the desire to know. The acquisition of knowledge is possible to the degree that men and women are willing to believe each other.[53] What each of us knows through immanently generated knowledge is minimal compared to the knowledge we have based on belief. In short, the appropriation of 'one's social, cultural, religious heritage is largely a matter of belief.'[54] Knowledge progresses because each successive generation takes what it has been given, adds to it through its own intellectual operations, and hands it on to the next generation. 'Human knowledge, then, is not some individual possession but rather a common fund, from which each may draw by believing, to which each may contribute in the measure that he performs his cognitional operations properly and reports their results accurately.'[55] Taylor does not explicitly work out an account of the nature of belief. Nonetheless, through his critique of a form of epistemology that seeks clarity and precision, 'the confidence that underlies this whole operation is that certainty is something we can generate for ourselves by ordering our thoughts correctly – according to clear and distinct connections,'[56] Taylor shows how my 'self-understanding necessarily has temporal depth and incorporates narrative,'[57] which are tacit judgments of belief. In short, the role of beliefs and the act of believing are an integral part of our acquisition of knowledge. In Heidegger's terminology we find ourselves 'thrown' into an already constituted set of meanings and values, most of which we believe. Because belief plays such a prominent role in our acquisition of knowledge, the real issue is not whether systematic doubt is the way one should proceed, but how one ought critically to control belief. Simply put, how is belief criticized?

Lonergan and Taylor, each in his own way, have given us an account of the source of mistaken beliefs. They 'have their roots in the scotosis of the dramatic subject, in the individual, group, and general bias of the practical subject, in the counterpositions of philosophy, and in their ethical implications and consequences.'[58] The critique of beliefs begins from 'the conviction that one has made one bad mistake, and it proceeds along the structural lines of one's own mentality and through the spontaneous and cumulative operations of the mind that alone can deal successfully with concrete issues.'[59] The problem of mistaken beliefs lies more within the believer. The believer must root out whatever bias infects her capacity to judge the valuableness or worthwhileness of any belief. Taylor likens this move to a Platonic *periagoge*, a turning of the soul's understanding from darkness to light. To quote Taylor, 'This is, I believe, the commonest form of practical reasoning in our lives, where we propose to our interlocutors transitions mediated by such error-reducing moves, by the identification of contradiction, the dissipation of confusion, or by rescuing from (usually motivated) neglect of considerations whose significance they cannot contest.'[60] For Lonergan, this rooting out is explicitly manifested in the morally converted subject giving free reign to the full dynamic operations of conscious intentionality.

There is another element to the issue of knowledge from above downwards, which has to do with religious conversion and the faith that follows from being in love with the divine ground. To quote Taylor, 'With the right direction of love, things become evident which are hidden otherwise.'[61]

Generally speaking, most of us are born into a given religious tradition. So in many ways we find ourselves thrown into a context of religious values and meanings. These meanings and values are carried intersubjectively, artistically, symbolically, linguistically, or in the 'remembered and portrayed lives or deeds or achievements of individuals or classes or groups.'[62] In sum, religion enters the world 'mediated by meaning and regulated by value. It endows that world with its deepest meanings and its highest value. It sets itself in a context of other meanings and other values. Within that context it comes to understand itself, to relate itself to the object of ultimate concern, to draw on the power of ultimate concern to pursue the objectives of proximate concern all the more fairly and all the more efficaciously.'[63]

Faith is knowledge born of religious love. 'Faith reveals the object of my religious love, directing me to discern how to develop a more perfect communion and union with the 'transcendent unknown other' who has entered into my conscious being and dwells within me in some mysterious way.'[64] For Lonergan, the experience of faith is the experienced fulfilment of the dynamic orientation of consciousness in its unrestrictedness. The experienced fulfilment of that 'thrust in its unrestrictedness may be objec-

tified as a clouded revelation' the intelligibility that grounds all intelligibility, the truth that grounds all truth, the goodness that grounds all
goodness, and the holiness that grounds all holiness.[65]

Taylor, in *A Catholic Modernity?* likewise claims that the experience of
faith is the acknowledgment of the transcendent. To acknowledge this
'means being called to a change of identity.'[66] Faith can be seen as a 'calling for a radical de-centering of the self in relation with God.'[67] In a more
Christian voice, Taylor understands this nascent experience of religious
conversion as a grasp of our being in the image of God. This 'being in the
image of God is also our standing among others in the stream of love,
which is that facet of God's life we try to grasp,'[68] albeit inadequately. Conversely, a truncated humanism can close off the window to the transcendent by suggesting there is nothing higher or beyond our deepest longing,
and this Augustinian restlessness is really a form of pathology.[69]

Faith, as the expression of religious conversion, can be linked to development individually, socially, culturally, and historically, and it meets the
problem of decline. Faith 'reveals an ultimate significance in human
achievement; it strengthens new undertakings with confidence. Inversely,
progress realizes the potentialities of man and of nature; it reveals that
man exists to bring about an ever fuller achievement in this world; and that
achievement because it is man's good also is God's glory.'[70] Finally, just as
belief in general is the result of a judgment of value, the value that faith
uncovers is the value of believing and accepting the word of religion, its
judgments of value, and its judgments of facts.[71] As Taylor suggests, 'Here's
where the foregrounding of feeling, and the moment of conversion and
inspiration, take him away from the kind of religious life that may start in a
moment of blinding insight, but then continues through some, perhaps
very demanding discipline.'[72]

Taylor consistently maintains that within the subject there is an eros, an
aspiration to wholeness that is, to use Lonergan's term, the operator that
moves the subject to self-transcendence. Moreover, our desire for completion is not a misplaced desire that is put forward onto a neutral cosmos.
Rather, there is something beyond us that calls us forward; this is somewhat analogous to Heidegger's 'call of conscience.' 'If authenticity is being
true to ourselves, is recovering our own *sentiment de l'existence*, then perhaps
we can only achieve it integrally if we recognize that this sentiment connects us to a wider whole.'[73] In other words, one's identity can be constituted truthfully only within a context of something that matters. 'To
bracket out history, nature, society, the demands of solidarity, everything
but what I find in myself, would be to eliminate all candidates for what
matters.'[74] From Lonergan's perspective this approach of Taylor's is
nascently an expression of moral conversion whereby the subject begins to

ask questions regarding the worthwhileness or valuableness of a given course of action. For Taylor, 'a person is a being with a certain moral status ... but underlying the moral status, as its condition, are certain practices. A person is a being who has a sense of self, has a notion of the future and the past, can hold values, make choices, in short can adopt life-plans, which implies that we make moral and value judgments about his life.'[75] Taylor argues that this capacity for adopting life plans takes place within a context of higher and lower ways of living out one's life. We make 'qualitative contrasts,' which suggests that one way of living is higher than others, 'or in other cases that a certain way of living is debased.'[76]

This higher goal is distinguished from what Taylor calls ordinary goals. These ordinary goals are such things as wealth or comfort. Obtaining these things involves certain utilitarian steps; however, if someone lacks wealth, there is usually no condemnation for its lack. On the other hand, the question of a higher goal suggests that one ought to have this and failure to do so can lead to some form of condemnation, because to recognize something as a higher goal is to recognize it as one that all ought to follow.[77] As human agents, there is a normative demand placed upon us to 'perspicuously articulate' what that higher ideal must be, and how we are to be in contact with it. In addition, within the context of our heritage, we ought to be able to make discriminating judgments about what is worthwhile for us and for others.

As Lonergan has pointed out, the heritage that is the source of this ideal is rarely if ever free from distortion.[78] While Taylor recognizes the existence of rights and a moral horizon out of which we struggle to live authentically; nonetheless, once 'we are within the hermeneutic circle of engaged human agency, there can be no external criterion of judgment for our articulation to correspond to whether accurately or otherwise. For any attempt to establish such correspondence is a naive attempt to escape the circle we are always already engaged in – the very circle that confers intelligibility upon our interpretations and without which our articulations cannot be perspicuous.'[79]

To repeat, Taylor sees modern epistemology making claims about knowledge that are illusory. 'It assumes wrongly that we can get to the bottom of what knowledge is, without drawing on our never fully articulate understanding of human life and experience.'[80] The rise of the notion of reason as disengaged, powerful, controlling, and possessing an unchallenged clarity not only flies in the face of human experience, but leads to a pernicious form of subjectivism. Taylor, to counteract this disengaged view of reason, uses hermeneutics and his analysis of weak and strong evaluations to show that not only do we make crucial qualitative distinctions between things of worth, but also these evaluations are about things that exist independently of us. 'Authenticity is clearly self-referential: this has to be my orientation. But this doesn't mean that on another level the content must be self-referential: that my goals must express or fulfill my desires or aspirations, as against something that stands beyond these. I can find fulfillment in God, or a political cause, or tending the earth. Indeed, the argument above suggests that we will find genuine fulfillment only in something like this, which has significance independent of us or our desires.'[81]

The Question of Foundation

Again, Taylor is acutely aware of the problem of epistemological foundationalism as an approach to human subjectivity; as a result, he ends up grounding his notion of authenticity and his analysis of human intentionality in our common cultural heritage. This social teleology is the horizon in which one finds one's ideal of authenticity. 'We have already become something. Questions of truth and freedom can arise for us in the transformations we undergo or project. In short, we have a *history*. We live in time not just self-enclosed in the present, but essentially related to a past which has helped define our identity, and a future which puts it again in question.'[82] There is also the fact that in real radical choice we have to 'in some sense experience the pull' of the various choices and give our assent;[83] Taylor seems to locate the fulfilment of our desire for wholeness within a social teleology, which in turn offers an array of possibilities already constitutive of the community's self-understanding. Because he takes seriously the fact that one can no longer speak of a normative human nature in the old metaphysical sense – 'what was once so solid has in many cases melted into air shows that we are dealing not with something grounded in the nature of being, but rather with changeable human interpretations'[84] – he is now constrained to make his case in terms of a hermeneutics of objects.[85] Yet concepts and ideals such as dignity, freedom, justice, liberty, and equality are ambiguous. At most, their meaning is a matter of not yet thematized possibilities that await further insights, decisions, and choices to render them intelligible and concrete.[86] Taylor sees hermeneutical understanding as our ability to 'think together' and realizes that language enables us 'to articulate or make manifest the background of distinctions of worth we define ourselves by.'[87] I think Taylor's approach to hermeneutical understanding, while important, is somewhat abbreviated, because it does not seem to get at 'precise speech about the intelligible in the sensible and insights into concrete situations.'[88] For instance, in Taylor's reply to Rorty in *Philosophy in an Age of Pluralism*, he writes, 'What is needed is not a Davidsonian "principle of clarity" ... but rather coming to understand that there is a very different way of understanding human life, the cosmos, the holy etc. Somewhere along the line you need some place in your ontology for something like the Aztec way of seeing things.'[89] What Taylor is calling for is a pluralism of meaning that takes seriously the richness of the human world mediated by a constitutive form of common-sense meaning whereby the person 'constitutes not only his social institutions and their cultural significance but also the story of the world's shape and origin and destiny.'[90] This is important for Taylor, because of the need to overcome a certain cover story coming out of the Enlightenment that only the rigors of science gives us truth of the empirical world, and that such things as an Aztec cosmology are to be relegated to the infantile past of human existence. Taylor wants us to take seriously the fact that human beings are symbolic and linguistic animals and it is through symbols 'that mind and body, mind and heart, heart and body communicate.'[91] Yet in this instance, Taylor's genuine concern for the validity and realism of the plurality of meanings falls short of being able to adequately differentiate between a world mediated by common-sense meaning, and a world mediated by scientific meanings. For example, when Taylor talks about Kepler's achievement as a 'new description, a shift to a new scheme ... which allowed a superior description in virtue of what we now recognize to be features of the universe,'[92] it is difficult, given Taylor's 'way of seeing things,' how he could argue for the superior position of Kepler's account of planetary ellipses, vis-à-vis an Aztec cosmology. But Lonergan's hermeneutics of cognitional interiority is able to facilitate such a move. In Lonergan's account of cognitional theory and the event of insight, one is able to talk about the 'intelligible in the sensible and insight into concrete situations.' Lonergan draws the distinction between explanation and description. Description is an account of something as it appears to me: colour, heavy/light, strong/soft, and so forth. An explanatory account, conversely, prescinds from how something appears to me (Galileo's mistake regarding primary and secondary qualities) to give an account of the intelligible relationship that exists within the data. Let me quote at length from Joseph Flanagan's *Quest for Self-Knowledge*:

> They [human beings] also operate in practical, common-sense schemes of knowing, which place knowers within a world related to themselves and to others in and through descriptive patterns of experience. To enter the world of theory, human knowers have to learn how to decenter themselves and recenter themselves within strictly explanatory patterns of knowing that correlate things to one another ... Human knowers, then, live in the immediate world of sensible objects which they mediate symbolically, linguistically, pragmatically, and theoretically. The epistemological problem is to differentiate

these patterns from one another and appropriate the various worlds of objects to which they orient us.[93]

Moreover, Lonergan's phenomenological account of consciousness shows that it is a dynamic structure that wants insights that are intelligent, rational, and responsible. Asking questions is not enough. We want to know whether what we think or believe is true, is in fact the case, whether what we value and choose is what is truly worthwhile, or whether the true object of our affection is not just illusory. The dynamic orientation of human being already has a notion of the intelligibility, goodness, valuableness, absoluteness, unconditionedness, and loveableness of being. 'In other words, there is at work in our questions a primordial meaning (Ur-Sinn) in search of the intelligible, the true, the real, a primordial meaning that is a priori because it constitutes the "stuff" of the human spirit itself.'[94] This sets the context for my second point. If, as Lonergan suggests, one's heritage is rarely free from aberration because of the consistent presence of different types of biases, how is one ever to adequately address the problem of appropriating an ideal that in some ways continues to be distorted?

Taylor addresses this problem in terms of the dialogical nature of human beings: 'The general feature of human life that I want to evoke is its fundamentally dialogical character. We become full human agents, capable of understanding ourselves, and hence of defining an identity, through our acquisition of rich human languages of expression.'[95] In 'Transcendental Arguments' he stresses the importance of moving from sketchier to richer descriptions of experience. Yet as we try to formulate more clearly our experiences, we find that at times these formulations can further distort what we are trying to clarify: 'The deeper we go, that is, and the richer the description, the more a cavil can be raised.'[96] He concedes that while transcendental arguments are foundational because they articulate the point of our action and seek clarity, 'they must articulate what is most difficult for us to articulate, and so are open to endless debate.'[97] Taylor's dialogical approach, while in many ways normative, is not sufficiently differentiated in order to face the problem of authentically eliminating inauthenticity in the way Lonergan does when he writes, 'But it is only as they become aware of all bias in themselves, only as they sedulously guard against all its manifestations, only then can they be genuinely open to others and really effective in coming to know them in truth and justice.'[98] True, Taylor is very much aware of the problem of self-deception and admits that any genuine dialogue is always circumscribed by the possible presence of this fact. There is for Taylor something of a prior virtue that needs to be in place in order to overcome the problem of self-deception: it is 'openness,' the *apeiron* that the slave boy exhibited in Plato's dialogue *Meno.* But Taylor is not as clear as one would hope in trying to account for how, if the tradition itself has become corrupted, one can do more than genuinely appropriate the disingenuous. Even if one sincerely and genuinely engages in a dialogue with the other, who also is genuinely concerned with the truth of the matter, if the heritage that forms the context of their discussion is itself distorted, the interlocutors can only appropriate what has been distorted. 'Even if anyone manages to be perfectly authentic in all his own personal performance, still he cannot but carry within himself the ballast of his tradition. And down the millennia in which that tradition developed, one can hardly exclude the possibility that unauthenticity entered in and remained to ferment the mass through ages to come.'[99] Even with Taylor's account of epiphanic art as a disclosure of something noble or courageous that calls me out of myself, there is still the question of how one is to critically control the meaning of those types of events. We know that art, literature, music, and religious symbolism have been used to promote other ends besides the moral development of humanity. In an article on Nazi art James Fenton writes, 'Hitler's face [referring to the work by Hubert Lanzinger, *The Color Bearer*, which shows Hitler riding in shining armour] has been attacked with some sharp object, but it seems to be thought inappropriate to restore Nazi art – it will remain defaced, as a tribute to the feared power of their image.'[100]

From Lonergan's perspective, the solution to the problem of 'the truth of existence' lies, in principle, in what he sees as an invariant pattern of human knowing: the general empirical method. This method takes seriously not only the data of sense and the data of consciousness, but also the temporal constitutiveness of the human being, without capitulating to their vicissitudes. In other words, Lonergan's general empirical method takes to heart the postmodern turn that protests any kind of exclusive absoluteness that closes off the question of a plurality of other possibilities.[101] It does this by emphasizing the central importance of contingency in the judgments we make, 'that every event ... is conditional and conditioned ... So our human judgments possess that odd combination of normativity, fallibility and possible revisability.'[102] The attainment of self-transcendence in terms of the 'truth of existence' involves a slow and laborious development and maturation that moves from below upwards, and from above downwards. 'Teaching, and learning, investigating, coming to understand ... these are not independent of the subject of times and places, of psychological, social, historical conditions.'[103] Lonergan's hermeneutics of human nature does not posit a 'disengaged subject,' or claim the power and control that Taylor associates with Cartesian clarity. Rather, Lonergan thinks that this odd form of normativity may be attained by obeying the exigencies of conscious operations. 'The intelligence in each of us prompts us to seek understanding, to be dissatisfied with a mere glimmer, to keep probing for an ever fuller grasp, to pin down in accurate expressions just what we have attained.'[104] Through his cognitional theory Lonergan has not only differentiated more clearly than Taylor the erotic nature of human being, he has given us a stronger account of an invariant form of engaged agency that might help us out of a vicious hermeneutical circle: 'It is the operative intentional foundations, prior to analysis, conceptualization, and judgment that are properly invariant.'[105]

Lonergan's own hermeneutical analysis of the dynamic structure of consciousness shows that the orientation of human existence to self-realization is attained only by unfailing fidelity to transcendental precepts: be attentive, be intelligent, be reasonable, be responsible, and be loving.[106] These precepts refer to the dynamic orientation and operations of consciousness: to be attentive means to be spontaneously aware of the wide range of our sensate and affective responses to a given situation. To be intelligent means we are never satisfied with partial answers. We are aware of our failures in understanding and strive to convey exactly what we think we have understood. Being reasonable is to demand sufficient evidence for our judgments and ways of proceeding. 'Our reasonableness demands sufficient evidence, marshals and weighs all it can find, is bound to assent when evidence is sufficient and may not assent when it is insufficient.'[107] To be responsible is to deliberate, decide, and act according to value and not just satisfaction. Responsibility is the 'reasonableness of action. Just as we cannot be reasonable and pass judgment beyond or against the evidence, so too we cannot be responsible without adverting to what is right and what is wrong.'[108] Lastly, when we are in love we spontaneously operate not for ourselves alone, but for the good of the other. We want what is valuable and worthwhile for ourselves and the other. If the exigencies of human consciousness are left unfettered, and not controlled or distorted by power or any bias, then the mystery that we are will be allowed to reveal itself in and through being. As Fred Lawrence points out, the framework for self-transcendence is this universe that 'gives an even more radically decentering or eccentric twist to the conscious subject, because the concrete evolution of 'that opaque and luminous being' is swept up ... into a vertical finality that is at once possible, multivalent, obscure, and indeed mysterious.'[109] To quote Lonergan, 'Such vertical finality is another name for self-transcendence. By experience we attend to the other; by understanding we gradually construct our world; by judgment we discern its independence of ourselves; by deliberate and responsible freedom we move beyond merely self-regarding norms and make ourselves moral beings.'[110]

Lonergan and Taylor take seriously the inner exigencies of the subject, which, in Taylor's terminology, indexes us to what is other. Where Taylor's emphasis falls primarily upon a hermeneutics of objects and its relationship to the eros of the human spirit, Lonergan is more explicit in claiming that the eros of the human spirit is intrinsically ordered to the *true*, the *good*, and the *holy*. While the meanings of these terms are articulated culturally, the person's dynamic orientation to the above transcendentals, if given free reign, pushes the human subject beyond the limited expressions constituted culturally. In short, both understand that there is a normative orientation to engaged agency that stands dialectically to contingent realization. 'So the many levels of consciousness are just successive stages in the unfolding of a single thrust, the eros of the human spirit. To know the good, it must know the real; to the real, it must know the true; to know the true, it must know the intelligible; to know the intelligible, it must attend to the data.'[111]

The Human Good

It is now worthwhile to revisit Lonergan's notion of value, and Taylor's concept of hypergoods. For Taylor, the question of why one has chosen this good, value, or hypergood, as opposed to others, cannot be settled according to a criterion, because from Taylor's perspective a criterion suggests that one follows a rule or a natural science methodology. The problem with this way of thinking about our choices is that it militates against the fact that our account of the world in which we live is 'essentially that of an embodied agent, engaged with or at grips with the world.'[112] To see practical reason as rule-following is to place the criteria outside lived experience. In other words, to give an account of one's choice concerning what is good or valuable, or one's overarching hypergood, is to engage in an act of practical reasoning that Taylor calls the *best account principle*. This form of practical reasoning is a hermeneutics of engagement. It is the way in which we try to make sense of our lives. For Taylor, practical reasoning, then, is neither utilitarian nor a form of naturalism whereby one must get at the criteria for one's decisions. Rather, practical reasoning is a reasoning about transitions from one position A to new position B. Practical reasoning 'aims to establish, not that some position is correct absolutely, but rather that some position is superior to some other.'[113] Practical reasoning, therefore, is concerned with comparative evaluations: 'We show one of these comparative claims to be well founded when we can show that the *move* from A to B constitutes a gain epistemically.'[114] To gain epistemically means that a transition argument is an error-reducing argument. I come to realize, for instance, that my earlier account of justice was excessively narrow. The shift from position A to position B posits the claim that position B is the superior and more valid account because I have gained greater purchase on the meaning of this term both culturally and individually. This claim is not the result of rule-following or some other external criteria.

In other words, transitional arguments, which are comparative claims about the worthwhileness of competing values, have their 'source in biographical narrative.'[115] Rather, 'we are convinced that a certain view is superior because we have *lived* a transition which we understand as error-reducing and hence as epistemic gain'[116] (my emphasis). It is not to be suggested, however, that transition claims are therefore immune to further clarification. Quite the contrary, 'our conviction that we have grown morally can be challenged by another. It may, after all, be illusion. And then we argue; and arguing here is contesting between interpretations of what I have been living.'[117] In addition, if, in the context of the struggle to be authentic, hypergoods arise so as to revalue earlier commitments, 'the conviction they carry comes from our reading of the transitions to them, from a certain understanding of moral growth.'[118] One of the issues at stake here in this transition to hypergoods, as well as moral reasoning in general, is the account of the order of argument. In a faulty form of moral reasoning one invokes realities that stand outside the context of the disputed interpretations. One starts with something like 'the Good' or God and then works one's way back to what ought to be done.[119] The problem with this approach is not with the Good or God. Rather, it is the assumption that these hypergoods stand outside the context of a lived narrative. Any discussion of hypergoods, or moral ontology in general, must be given in 'anthropocentric terms, terms which relate to the meanings things have for us, then the demand to start outside of all such meanings, not to rely on our moral intuitions or on what we find morally moving, is in fact a proposal to change the subject.'[120] Certainly there is nothing preventing us from seeing God or the Good as foundational to our understanding of our self and our world. But our acceptance of any hypergood is not because it stands outside or is independent of our lived moral experience. Rather, our apprehension of the worthwhileness of a particular hypergood is grounded in a complex experience of being *moved* by it.[121] 'We sense in the very experience of being moved by some higher good that we are moved by what is good in it rather than that it is valuable because of our reaction. We are moved by seeing its point as something infinitely valuable. We experience our love for it as a well-founded love. Nothing that couldn't move me in *this* way would count as a hypergood.'[122] This experience of being moved and being in love is Taylor's nascent account of moral conversion. Again as with any good or value, the question of whether one is right or not is predicated upon whether one raises the relevant questions and faces this or that particular critique.[123] Taylor eschews any discussion of criteria, which he associates with naturalism and utilitarianism, for a moral ontology that is anthropocentric. 'The most reliable moral view is not one that would be grounded quite outside our intuitions but one that is grounded on our strongest intuitions, where these have successfully met the challenge of proposed transitions away from them.'[124]

Finally, Taylor claims that any discussion concerning hypergoods is unsettling because ideals of this kind rank above 'the recognized goods of the society; it can in some cases challenge and reject'[125] the other goods. Whatever ideal claims our allegiance makes us re-evaluate other goods within our horizon. According to one of Nietzsche's critiques, talk about a highest good or hypergood gives licence to reject the putatively 'lower' in us as human beings.[126] Hence, neo- Nietzscheans speak of hypergoods as forms of oppression and exclusion. While Taylor acknowledges this disconcerting element to hypergoods, he insists one cannot live without some overarching ideal, although he asserts that we have 'to search for a way in which our strongest aspirations towards hypergoods do not exact a price of self-mutilation.'[127] Yet it would be a major mistake to exclude a good because of the possibility that it might lead to some form of suffering or loss.[128]

Like Taylor, Lonergan also shows how feelings are intentionally related to values. Feelings are not only an intentional response to values, they also respond 'in accord with some scale of preferences.' Where Taylor differentiates only between weak and strong evaluations, and hyper and ordinary goods, Lonergan maintains we may intelligently distinguish between 'vital, social, cultural, personal, and religious values in ascending order.'[129]

In general, to intend the human good is to respond to not only values but also a process that is both personal and social. Lonergan shows that higher values condition the lower, and the realization of the lower values conditions the possibility of distinguishing the scale of preference for the various values. In other words, vital values such as one's strength and health are normally preferred in spite of the work, privations, and self-sacrifices involved in acquiring, maintaining, and restoring them. For instance, consistent cardiovascular exercise, in spite of the inconvenience or pain, is to be preferred over not doing anything and placing one's health at risk. Social values, such as the good of order, which conditions the vital values of the whole community, have to be preferred to the vital values of the individual members of the community. Lonergan uses the homey example of breakfast to illustrate the point. If breakfast is an important good for me in maintaining the vital values of health and stamina, for example, chances are it is good for many others of the community. As a result, a system is devised to ensure the ongoing recurrence of this good and hence the realization and maintenance of the vital value. To say that social values condition the vital is merely to point out that an individual's vital well-being should not override the concern for the well-being of others. My need to be physically protected in a community should not be at the expense of denying the same kind of protection to others. However, one does not live by bread alone. The need for something richer and more meaningful gives rise to cultural values. Cultural values do not and cannot exist without the realization of vital and social values; nonetheless, cultural values rank higher in the scale of preference. 'Over and above mere living and operating, men have to find a meaning and value in their living and operating. It is the function of culture to discover, express, validate, criticize, correct, develop, improve such meaning and value.'[130]

From cultural values one moves upward to personal values. Personal value is existential self-transcendence. It is the subject choosing and deciding what is truly worthwhile, what is truly valuable, and in accord with the scale of preference. Personal value means the human being is a self-transcending subject who originates value in herself and her milieu. In turn, existential self-transcendence opens the subject up to the true quest of life, the intention of religious value: the top of the scale.[131] In sum, the scale of preference in values reflects the levels of transcendence of the intentional subject: experiencing, understanding, judging, deciding, and loving.

Not only is the scale of values somewhat isomorphic to the subject, one can see in the scale of values an interlocking relationship of conditioning to conditioned that moves from below upwards and from above downwards: the two vectors of the 'hermeneutical circle.' 'The vital values of a community are contingent upon the good of order, a social system that demands contributions on the part of the subject that go beyond procuring one's own vital values. Thus social values call for a more self-transcending response than do vital values.'[132] However, one's social order is always an order constituted by meaning; there is, then, more to human living than just the realization of vital values. Thus cultural values, while dependent upon vital and social values, rank higher. 'Over and above mere living and operating, men have to find a meaning and value in their living and operating. It is the function of culture to discover, express, validate, criticize, correct, develop, improve such meaning and value.'[133] Pursuit of cultural values calls the subject beyond merely a practical, common-sense concern with the social. In addition, through cultural values one is able to criticize and correct the meanings and values that constitute a given social order, but only to the extent the person is being attentive, intelligent, reasonable, responsible, and loving: authentic. This, then, is personal value. Finally, sustained authenticity is impossible without growth in a loving relationship fully brought to fruition by being in love with the source of all meaning and value. 'To be in love is to be in love with someone. To be in love without qualifications or conditions or reservations or limits is to be in love with someone transcendent ... In the measure that summit is reached, then the supreme value is God, and other values are God's expression of his love in this world, in its aspirations, and in its goal.'[134]

According to Robert Doran, the order of conditioning is inverse to the order of differentiation. The order of differentiation moves from vital to social to cultural to personal and finally religious. However, the order of conditioning moves from above downward. 'The realization of religious values is the condition of authenticity. Authenticity is the condition of genuine cultural values. Cultural values are the condition of a just social order. And a just social order is the condition of the realization of the vital values of the whole community.'[135] Where Taylor shows how one intelligently chooses a hypergood by distinguishing between weak and strong affective evaluations, Lonergan's account shows that the scale of preference constitutes an objective order by which one is able to determine the degree of one's participation in the concrete process of realizing the human good. 'The objectivity of the order is constituted by the self-transcendence to which the subject attains in responding to the different values.'[136] The determining factor of the quality of the context of one's judgments of value is whether one grows or backslides in the domain of personal value.[137] By Taylor's account, if 'hypergoods arise through supersessions, the conviction they carry comes from our reading of the transitions to them, from a certain understanding of moral growth.'[138] With Lonergan the 'immanent order of our intentionality is the source and criterion of human authenticity and of cognitive and moral objectivity.'[139] Because much of what we claim to know and value is based on belief, and this belief coupled to our own immanently generated knowledge of fact and value constitutes our heritage, the one fundamental decision that a 'maturing adult is called upon to make is the question of the stance that is to be taken towards one's heritage itself, and indeed this question may be said to be the most basic of all human judgments of value and decisions. It is the option where major authenticity is at stake.'[140]

Lonergan beyond Taylor

Contrary to neo-Nietzschean critiques, authentic self-transcendence is anything but mutilating, because the values we respond to are in accord with a scale of preference. Moreover, intellectual, moral, and religious conversion all has to do with being-a-whole-self. When all three conversions are present within a single consciousness 'it is possible to conceive their relations in terms of sublation.'[141] Lonergan's use of the term *sublation* is not that of Hegel. Sublation does not destroy what is sublated, but 'introduces something new and distinct, puts everything on a new basis ... includes it, preserves all its proper features and properties and carries them forward to a fuller realization within a richer context.'[142] Thus moral conversion, far from destroying intellectual conversion that reorients the search for truth, reorients the subject from satisfactions to values. The subject is, in Lonergan's words, 'established as an originating value.' The subject's orientation to the truth is strengthened not only because of the subject's need to correctly apprehend reality, but also because of the further need to respond to the real possibilities of actualizing values. Finally, just as moral conversion sublates, enriches, and enhances intellectual conversion, religious conversion brings to complete fulfilment the eros of the human spirit. Religious conversion transforms the existential subject into a subject in love, a subject held, grasped, possessed, and owned through a total and so an other-worldly love. There is a new basis for all valuing and all doing good. In no way are fruits of intellectual or moral conversion negated or diminished. On the contrary, all human pursuits of the true and the good are included within and furthered by a cosmic context and purpose and, as well, there now accrues to man the power of love to enable him to accept the suffering involved in undoing the effects of decline.[143]

The problem of overcoming a heritage that is more often than not a mixture of authenticity and inauthenticity remains unsettled. For Lonergan, the solution to the problem lies not in the unravelling of the tradition, but in unmasking all forms of self-deception.

> The cure is not the undoing of tradition, for that is beyond our
> power. It is only through socialization, acculturation, education that
> we come to know that there is such a thing as tradition ... However
> much we react, criticize, endeavor to bring about change, the change
> itself will always be just tradition ... The issue is not tradition, for as
> long as men survive there will be tradition, rich or impoverished,
> good and evil.[144]

If unravelling the tradition is not the solution (and certainly for Taylor this is not an option), then what is needed is a thicker and more differentiated explanation of the experience of self-transcendence, one that not only complements Taylor's more undifferentiated account, but thematizes more concretely the 'human subject as subject.'[145] This Lonergan has done with his explication of the full range of the experience of self-transcendence. In fact, experiences of self-transcendence are almost commonplace. For instance, Ludwig Binswanger spoke of the shift from dreams of the night to dreams of the morning. Dreams of the night are largely influenced by 'somatic determinants such as the state of one's digestion. But in dreams of the morning the subject is anticipating his waking state; however fragmentary the dream and however symbolic its content, he is anticipating his world and taking his own stance within it.'[146] There is the acquisition of language where the child moves from a realm of sensory immediacy to a world mediated by meaning and motivated by value. The person 'moves out of the habitat of an animal and into the universe that adds the distant to what is near, the past and future to what is present, the possible and the probable to what is actual.'[147] Again there is the experience of transcendence manifested in the intentional operations of human consciousness as propelled by the questions we ask: What is it? Is it true? Is it worthwhile? Should I do it? These questions promote self-transcendence not because they move us out of a Kantian sphere of transcendental subjectivity to objects that are already-out-there-now-real: 'self-transcendence heads us towards *being*, and within the realm of being there are various individual beings ... to which the difference of subject and object belongs.'[148] It is, however, the experience of falling in love (the movement from above downwards) that is the framework for the de-centred and self-transcendent subject.[149] More specifically, it is falling in love with the divine ground (which comes as gift) that has the potential to add a deeper and much richer understanding of self-transcendence and is the solution to the problem of the distorted tradition. In other words, what one now apprehends in this experience of other worldly love is transcendental value, the ground of all value.[150] This intention of transcendental value opens one up to deeper levels of meaning and richer possibilities for the vital, social, cultural, and personal values. Knowledge born out of love of God places all other values in the light of transcendental value. Without knowledge born of religious love, the person becomes the only originating value, and the human good exhausts terminal value. But the human good is always under construction and susceptible to distortion. Religious love realizes that the divine ground is *the* originating value and no less than the whole universe makes up terminal value. From this perspective, the human good is not abolished or mutilated; it is taken up into the all-encompassing good of the divine ground. Within the viewpoint of the human good, the relationship is confined to human beings and nature. The knowledge of religious love pushes one's concern beyond the restriction of 'man's world to God and his world.'[151] Then human development (human authenticity) is more deeply understood not only to be about skills and virtues but also holiness. Most importantly, the limits of human aspirations cease to be the grave.[152]

Conclusion

What then is authenticity? Authenticity for Taylor and Lonergan is the experience of a profound transfiguration in one's being and doing. 'It is a transformation of our stance towards the world and self, rather than simply the registering of external reality.'[1] Another term for this experience of transformation is conversion. In Lonergan, this experience of conversion is explicitly intellectual, moral, and religious. In Taylor, it is implicitly moral and religious. For both, however, this transformation rests on an inner conviction. For Lonergan, this inner conviction is absent in someone who is stubborn or driven by power, for this inner conviction is the fruit of conversion and it is the concrete principle of authentic self-transcendence. Taylor sees this inner conviction as authentic self-transcendence; it is expressed 'in choosing ourselves in the light of the infinite.'[2] There is a normativity to this inner conviction and it is tied to a fidelity to the inbuilt exigencies of the basic operations of knowing choosing and loving. Anyone intent on 'achieving self-transcendence is ever aware of shortcomings, while those that are evading the issue of self-realization are kept busy concealing the fact from themselves.'[3] Do I really want to know what in fact is so? Do I really want to be responsible in my deliberations and choices? In Lonergan, this inner conviction regards whether the norms of attentiveness, intelligence, reasonableness, responsibility, and loving have been satisfied or not.[4] In Taylor, the inner conviction that informs authentic living reveals that self-transcendence is so much a matter of an 'inner dynamism of human reality that one cannot but be aware when one is moving towards it and, on the other hand, one cannot but feel constrained to conceal the fact when one is evading the abiding imperative of what it is to be human.'[5] Authenticity for Lonergan and Taylor, then, is a way of living one's life in a new dimension.[6] It is not automatic. Too often persons are just the oppo-site. But it is the most empowering way of living, for it addresses our deep-est desire, and for both thinkers our deepest 'need and most prized achievement is authenticity.'[7]

In spite of some important differences that exist between the two think-ers, for both, authentic human existence is, in Lonergan's terminology, the result of a long-sustained exercise of being attentive, intelligent, reasonable, responsible, and loving; the fruit of this is progress both individually and communally. Progress results from our being our true selves, by being prin-ciples of originating value in observing the transcendental precepts. Being intelligent grasps 'hitherto unnoticed or unrealized possibilities.' Being rea-sonable acknowledges what would not work, while also recognizing what would most likely succeed. Being responsible moves one beyond what Tay-lor has criticized as instrumental reason that makes one's choices and deci-sion on the basis of 'short-term and long-term effects to one's self, one's group and other groups.'[8] As for inauthenticity, no amount of dialogue can change those who are irresponsible, unreasonable, inattentive, and obtuse. A 'civilization in decline digs its own grave with a relentless consistency. It cannot be argued out of its self-destructive ways, for argument has a theo-retical major premise, theoretical premises are asked to conform to matters of fact, and the facts of the situation are already distorted by actions that are irresponsible, inattentive, and unreasonable.'[9] The kind of situation that results from inauthenticity is not intelligible. It is the social surd. Dos-toyevsky has shown us how 'loathing and self-loathing, inspired by the very real evils of the world, fuel a projection of evil outward, a polarization between self and world, where all the evil is now seen to reside.'[10] Such a sit-uation yields nothing. The only solution, finally, is redemption.

For Lonergan and Taylor, the principle of redemption is self-sacrificing love: 'What will transform us [and the world] is an ability to love the world, ourselves [and God], to see it as good in spite of the wrong.'[11] To fall in love is to 'set up a new principle that has, indeed, its causes, conditions, occasions, but, as long as it lasts, provides the mainspring of one's desire and fear, hope and despair, joy and sorrow.'[12] To the degree any commu-nity becomes an authentic community of love, it will set the conditions for the possibility of making real and great personal sacrifices. Authentic self-transcendence can overcome and correct the objective absurdities that inauthenticity has brought into being.[13] Taylor and Lonergan agree with Augustine in holding the priority of love proceeding knowledge. It is being in love where 'things become evident which are hidden otherwise.'[14] The ultimate sin, then, is to close one's self off to grace. The 'person who is closed is in a vicious circle from which it is hard to escape.'[15] In short, the solution to the social surd/evil is a religious one.

What will sweep away the rationalizations that have become hardened in the tradition? Certainly not more reasoning, for reason itself has fallen under suspicion. The answer lies in the full flowering of the transcendental nature of human being. The fruit of authentic 'self-transcendence consists in a "yes" to an incomparable presence apprehended as beauty, meaning, truth, or goodness, this consent brings about joy, peace, detachment, and freedom.'[16] The fullness of what it means to be human resides in our longing for the wholeness that is brought to fulfilment in our falling in love with the Divine Other, who has grasped us first. As Pascal put the matter, we would not be seeking God if he had not already found us. When reason becomes ineffective, particularly in its misguided guise as instrumental, then it is only religious conversion, and faith as the knowledge born of religious love that can smash the economic, social, cultural, and psychological structures that egoism has constructed and exploited. What then is offered? It is the hope beyond hope that religion inspires. 'When finally the human situation seethes with alienation, bitterness, resentment, recrimination, hatred and mounting violence, what can retributive justice bring about but a duplication of the evils that already exist? Then what is needed is not retributive justice, but self-sacrificing love':[17] authentic human existence.

Notes

Introduction

1 Douglas Rossinow, *The Politics of Authenticity* (New York: Columbia University Press, 1998), 4.
2 See Lionel Trilling, *Sincerity and Authenticity* (Cambridge, MA: Harvard University Press, 1972), for an account of how in literature one sees the shift from the notion of sincerity as a moral idea to the idea of authenticity.
3 Charles Taylor, *Sources of the Self* (Cambridge, MA: Harvard University Press, 1989), 369.
4 Ibid., 376. A fuller account of Rousseau and Herder's contribution to the modern idea of authenticity will be given in chapter 1.
5 Taylor, *Sources of the Self,* 508.
6 Allessandro Ferrara, *Modernity and Authenticity* (Albany, NY: SUNY Press, 1993), 9.
7 Ibid., 19.
8 Theodor Adorno, *The Jargon of Authenticity* (Evanston, IL: Northwestern University Press, 1973), 5.
9 Ibid., 9.
10 Ibid., 11.
11 Ibid., 21.
12 Ibid., 22.
13 Ibid., 15.
14 Ibid., 17–18.
15 Ibid., 81.
16 Ibid., 18.
17 Ibid.
18 Ibid., 14.

19 Ibid., 46.
20 Ibid., 58.
21 Ibid., 67.
22 Ibid.
23 Ibid., 126.
24 Ibid., 127.
25 Rossinow, *The Politics of Authenticity*, 5.
26 Frederick Lawrence, 'The Hermeneutic Revolution and the Future of Theology,' in *Between the Human and the Divine*, ed. Andrzej Wiercinski (Toronto: Hermeneutic Press, 2002), 330.
27 Ibid.
28 Contingency, pluralism, and concern for the other are genuine concerns for both Taylor and Lonergan. It should be pointed out, however, that certain postmodern approaches to unmasking all forms of master narratives are locked into a permanent 'hermeneutics of suspicion' where one is unable to 'furnish criteria for figuring out the difference between disordered self-love and right-ordered self-love.' See Frederick Lawrence, 'The Fragility of Consciousness,' *Theological Studies* 54 (1993): 204. For those theorists who are entrenched in this form of intellectual suspicion, Lonergan and Taylor's questions concerning criteria and normativity will fall on deaf ears.
29 James Tully, 'Preface,' in *Philosophy in an Age of Pluralism* (Cambridge: Cambridge University Press, 1994), xiv.
30 Charles Taylor, *The Ethics of Authenticity* (Cambridge, MA: Harvard University Press, 1991), 39.
31 Bernard Lonergan, *Collection* (Montreal: Palm, 1967), 240.

Chapter 1: Martin Heidegger: The One Thing Needful

1 Frederick Lawrence, 'The Hermeneutic Revolution and the Future of Theology,' in *Between the Human and the Divine*, ed. Andrzej Wiercinski (Toronto: Hermeneutic Press, 2002), 349.
2 Ibid., 333. See van Buren for a further account of Augustine's influence on the development of Heidegger's thought.
3 John van Buren, *The Young Heidegger* (Bloomington: Indiana University Press, 1994), 63.
4 William J. Richardson, *Heidegger* (The Hague: Nijhoff, 1974), 34.
5 Charles B. Guignon, 'Heidegger's "Authenticity" Revisited,' *Review of Metaphysics* 38 (1984): 321–39.
6 Martin Heidegger, *Being and Time*, trans. John Macquarrie and Edward Robinson (New York: Harper and Row, 1962), 32. See van Buren, *The Young Heidegger*, 170, on the Augustinian roots of Heidegger's claim that Dasein is always an open question to itself.

7 Richardson, *Heidegger*, 47.

8 Ibid., 48.

9 Michael Zimmerman, *Eclipse of the Self* (Athens: Ohio University Press, 1986), 56.

10 van Buren, *The Young Heidegger*, 179.

11 Heidegger, *Being and Time*, 176.

12 Zimmerman, *Eclipse of the Self*, 44.

13 Heidegger, *Being and Time*, 312.

14 William B. Macomber, *The Anatomy of Disillusion* (Evanston, IL: Northwestern University Press, 1967), 84–5.

15 Heidegger, *Being and Time*, 234.

16 Richardson, *Heidegger*, 52.

17 Macomber, *Anatomy of Disillusion*, 42.

18 Richardson, *Heidegger*, 52.

19 Ibid.

20 Macomber, *Anatomy of Disillusion*, 33.

21 Ibid., 30.

22 Richardson, *Heidegger*, 56.

23 Guignon, 'Heidegger's "Authenticity" Revisited,' 324.

24 Richardson, *Heidegger*, 100.

25 Ibid.

26 Ibid.

27 Macomber, *Anatomy of Disillusion*, 38.

28 Ibid., 62–3.

29 Ibid., 43.

30 Ibid.

31 Ibid., 35.

32 Ibid., 38.

33 Ibid., 36.

34 Guignon, 'Heidegger's "Authenticity" Revisited,' 322.

35 Ibid., 331.

36 Macomber, *Anatomy of Disillusion*, 63.

37 Heideger, *Being and Time*, 329.

38 Macomber, *Anatomy of Disillusion*, 31.

39 Ibid., 32.

40 Richardson, *Heidegger*, 28.

41 Macomber, *Anatomy of Disillusion*, 31.

42 Ibid., 32.

43 Ibid., 211, 213.

44 Heidegger, *Being and Time*, 329.

45 Guignon, 'Heidegger's "Authenticity" Revisited,' 326.

46 Heidegger, *Being and Time*, 321.

47 Macomber, *Anatomy of Disillusion*, 101.
48 Ibid., 32.
49 Guignon, 'Heidegger's "Authenticity" Revisited, 331.
50 Heidegger, *Being and Time*, 275.
51 Macomber, *Anatomy of Disillusion*, 32.
52 Richardson, *Heidegger*, 37.
53 Macomber, *Anatomy of Disillusion*, 219.
54 Heidegger, *Being and Time*, 220.
55 Louis A. Sass, *Madness and Modernism* (New York: Harper Collins, 1992), 48. What I think fascinating here is that Sass uses the idea of Stimmung in his analysis of schizophrenia. Even in the case of mental illness, mood seems to be revelatory. 'At other times what astonished Renee and riveted her attention was not so much the absence of a normal sense of authenticity, emotional resonance, or functional meanings, but the very fact that objects existed at all – their Mere Being.'
56 Macomber, *Anatomy of Disillusion*, 78.
57 Ibid.
58 Ibid.
59 Ibid.
60 Richardson, *Heidegger*, 65.
61 Heidegger, *Being and Time*, 173.
62 Ibid., 175.
63 Ibid., 331.
64 Macomber, *Anatomy of Disillusion*, 118.
65 Heidegger, *Being and Time*, 68.
66 Ibid., 168.
67 Guignon, 'Heidegger's "Authenticity" Revisited,' 333.
68 Ibid., 334.
69 Heidegger, *Being and Time*, 239.
70 Ibid., 183.
71 Macomber, *Anatomy of Disillusion*, 83.
72 Heidegger, *Being and Time*, 309.
73 Ibid., 304.
74 Ibid., 355.
75 Ibid., 378.
76 Ibid., 313.
77 Ibid., 314.
78 Guignon, 'Heidegger's "Authenticity" Revisited,' 331.
79 Heidegger, *Being and Time*, 315.
80 Ibid., 318.
81 Ibid.
82 Ibid.

83 Ibid., 353.
84 Richardson, *Heidegger*, 84.
85 Guignon, 'Heidegger's "Authenticity" Revisited,' 324.
86 Macomber, *Anatomy of Disillusion*, 90.
87 Guignon, 'Heidegger's "Authenticity" Revisited,' 327.
88 Lawrence, 'Hermeneutic Revolution,' 336.
89 Ibid., 336.
90 Ibid.
91 Richardson, *Heidegger*, 90.
92 Guignon, 'Heidegger's "Authenticity" Revisited,' 337.
93 Macomber, *Anatomy of Disillusion*, 99.
94 Richardson, *Heidegger*, 92.
95 Zimmerman, *Eclipse of the Self*, 131.
96 Charles Guignon, 'History and Commitment in the Early Heidegger,' in *Heidegger: A Critical Reader*, ed. Hubert L. Dreyfus and Harrison Hall (Oxford: Blackwell, 1992), 139.
97 Richardson, *Heidegger*, 90–1. To quote Heidegger directly, 'The resoluteness in which Dasein comes back to itself, discloses current factical possibilities of authentic existing, and discloses them in terms of the heritage which that resoluteness, as thrown, takes over.' *Being and Time*, 435.
98 Heidegger, *Being and Time*, 448.
99 Guignon uses this approach in 'History and Commitment in the Early Heidegger.'
100 Peter Berkowitz, *Nietzsche: The Ethics of an Immoralist* (Cambridge, MA: Harvard University Press, 1995), 4. The quote is in reference to Nietzsche's work, yet it seems to be that it is very relevant to Heidegger's own endeavour.
101 Ibid., 28.
102 William Richardson, 'Heidegger's Fall,' *American Catholic Philosophical Quarterly* 69 (1995): 234.
103 Berkowitz, *Nietzsche*, 31.
104 Richardson, 'Heidegger's Fall,' 251.
105 Berkowitz, *Nietzsche*, 42.
106 Macomber, *Anatomy of Disillusion*, 99.
107 Guignon, 'Heidegger's "Authenticity" Revisited,' 336.

Chapter 2: Charles Taylor: Ethics and the Expressivist Turn

1 Alasdair MacIntyre, *After Virtue* (Notre Dame, IN: University of Notre Dame Press, 1984), 2.
2 Charles Taylor, *Sources of the Self* (Cambridge, MA: Harvard University Press, 1989), 3.
3 Ibid., 98.

4 Fergus Kerr, 'Taylor's Moral Ontology,' in *Charles Taylor*, ed. Ruth Abbey (Cambridge: Cambridge University Press, 2004), 91.

5 Taylor, *Sources of the Self*, 506.

6 Ibid., 511.

7 Taylor does not state specifically that he also is engaged in dialectic method; however, the way he juxtaposes linked but opposed positions in his uncovering what is true about this idea of human authenticity is what Lonergan has in mind when he talks of a method that is not only genetic, but dialectic as well.

8 Charles Taylor, 'Engaged Agency and Background in Heidegger,' in *The Cambridge Companion to Heidegger*, ed. Charles Guignon (Cambridge: Cambridge University Press, 1993), 218.

9 Ibid. Taylor defines *engagement* to mean 'the world of the agent is shaped by his or her form of life, or history or bodily essence.'

10 Charles B. Guignon, 'Heidegger's "Authenticity" Revisited,' *Review of Metaphysics* 38 (1984): 336.

11 Taylor, *Sources of the Self*, x.

12 Friedrich Nietzsche, *On the Advantage and Disadvantage of History for Life* (Indianapolis: Hackett, 1980), 19.

13 Christopher Lasch, *The Culture of Narcissism* (New York: Norton, 1991), 166–7. 'The cult of authenticity reflects the collapse of parental guidance and provides it with a moral justification. It confirms, and clothes in the jargon of emotional liberation, the parent's helplessness to instruct the child in the ways of the world or to transmit ethical precepts.'

14 The reader will have to settle for something of a cursory presentation of Taylor's archaeology of our modern identity. For those interested in a detailed analysis I would simply refer to Taylor's *Sources of the Self*.

15 Charles Taylor, *The Ethics of Authenticity* (Cambridge, MA: Harvard University Press, 1991), 25.

16 Ibid., 28.

17 Ibid, 27. Alessandro Ferrara, in *Modernity and Authenticity* (Albany, NY: SUNY Press, 1993), 113, maintains that Rousseau's idea of authenticity was ethical and not aesthetic.

18 Taylor, *Ethics of Authenticity*, 27.

19 Ibid., 28–9.

20 Ibid.

21 Ibid.

22 Ibid.

23 Ibid., 14. 'This individualism involves a centering on the self and a concomitant shutting out, or even unawareness, of the greater issues or concerns that transcend the self, be they religious, political, historical. As a consequence, life is narrowed or flattened.'

24 *Boosters* and *knockers* are Taylor's terms to designate both sides of the debate on the meaning of authenticity.

25 Taylor, *Ethics of Authenticity*, 23.

26 Ibid., 16.

27 Ibid., 17–18. 'Liberalism of neutrality' maintains that a political community must remain silent on the question what is the good life? To raise such a question invites the possibility of exclusion and possible repression of individuals or groups that fall outside the norm.

28 Charles Taylor, *Human Agency and Language* (Cambridge: Cambridge University Press, 1985), 35ff.

29 Taylor, *Ethics of Authenticity*, 34.

30 Charles Taylor, *Multiculturalism and the Politics of Recognition* (Princeton, NJ: Princeton University Press, 1992), 34.

31 Taylor, *Ethics of Authenticity*, 34.

32 Charles Taylor, *Philosophy and the Human Sciences* (Cambridge: Cambridge University Press, 1985), 258.

33 Ibid.

34 Ibid.

35 Taylor, *Sources of the Self*, 50.

36 Ibid., 36.

37 Ibid., 39.

38 Charles Taylor, 'Overcoming Epistemology,' in *After Philosophy*, ed. Kenneth Baynes, James Bohman, and Thomas McCarthy (Cambridge, MA: MIT Press, 1993), 476.

39 Taylor, *Sources of the Self*, 18. See also 'Engaged Agency and Background in Heidegger,' 325: 'When we find the Self, in a certain experience intelligible, what we are attending to, explicitly and expressly, is this experience. The context stands as the unexplicited horizon within which – or to very the image, as the vantage point from out of which – this experience can be understood.'

40 Ibid., 19.

41 Heidegger, *Being and Time*, 165.

42 Taylor, *Sources of the Self*, 26.

43 Taylor, *Human Agency and Language*, 3.

44 Taylor, *Sources of the Self*, 27.

45 Taylor, *Philosophy and the Human Sciences*, 236.

46 Taylor, *Human Agency and Language*, 35.

47 Taylor, *Ethics of Authenticity*, 39.

48 Ibid., 33.

49 Taylor, *Sources of the Self*, 34–5.

50 Taylor, *Human Agency and Language*, 8.

51 Taylor, *Sources of the Self*, 39. Taylor's use of the word *tradition* is what Heidegger

understands by a heritage: a reflective appropriation of those meanings and values that have shaped us in a particular way.

52 Charles Taylor, *Philosophical Arguments* (Cambridge, MA: Harvard University Press, 1995), 113.

53 Ibid., 96.

54 Ibid., 112.

55 Ibid., 106.

56 Nicholas H. Smith, 'Taylor and the Hermeneutic Tradition,' in *Charles Taylor*, ed. Ruth Abbey (Cambridge: Cambridge University Press, 2004), 39.

57 Ibid.

58 Nicholas Plants, 'Lonergan and Taylor,' *Method: Journal of Lonergan Studies* 19, no. 1 (2001): 149.

59 Ibid., 153.

60 Ibid., 157.

61 Taylor, *Sources of the Self*, 26.

62 Ibid., 31.

63 Frederick Lawrence, 'Lonergan: The Integral Post-Modern?' *Method: Journal of Lonergan Studies* 18, no. 2 (2000), 109.

64 This notion of the punctual self comes from Taylor's reading of Locke, Hobbes, and Descartes. All three thinkers posit the human person as ahistorical. For Descartes it is human reason severed from any natural orientation to a world independent of the self, or shaped by any prior judgments, insights not only of oneself but also one's community. For Locke and Hobbes, their 'State of Nature Stories' begin without any history of the person in this state. They just appear.

65 Taylor, *Sources of the Self*, 36.

66 Ibid.

67 Taylor, *Ethics of Authenticity*, 77.

68 Ibid., 13.

69 Ibid., 18.

70 Taylor, *Sources of the Self*, 362.

71 Taylor, *Multiculturalism*, 91.

72 Taylor, *Philosophical Arguments*, 23.

73 Ibid., 38.

74 Taylor, *Human Language and Agency*, 17.

75 Taylor, *Philosophical Arguments*, 41.

76 Taylor, *Sources of the Self*, 72.

77 Ibid.

78 Ibid.

79 Ibid.

80 Ibid., 450.

81 Ibid., 448.

82 Ibid.

83 Ibid., 72.

84 Ibid.

85 Ibid., 75.

86 Ibid., 72. Taylor's use of the term *anthropocentric* should not be equated with the 'subjectivism' he wants to argue against. The terms should be understood with respect to Taylor's account of engaged agency.

87 Bernard Lonergan, *Third Collection*, ed. Fred Crowe (New York: Paulist, 1985), 190–4. See also Eric Voegelin, *Plato and Aristotle*, vol. 3 of *Order and History* (Baton Rouge: Louisiana State University Press, 1957).

88 Taylor, *Sources of the Self*, 74.

89 Ibid.

90 Ibid., 75.

91 Frederick Lawrence, 'The Hermeneutic Revolution and the Future of Theology,' in *Between the Human and the Divine*, ed. Andrzej Wiercinski (Toronto: Hermeneutic Press, 2002).

92 Ibid.

93 Taylor, *Philosophical Arguments*, 69.

94 Ibid. In Taylor's essay 'To Follow a Rule,' he speaks of the background 'as really incorporating understanding; that is, as a grasp on things which although quite unarticulated may allow us to formulate reasons and explanations when challenged.' *Philosophical Arguments*, 168.

95 Taylor, *Sources of the Self*, 79. See also 53.

96 Ibid., 41.

97 Ibid., 42.

98 Charles Taylor, 'Critical Notice,' *Canadian Journal of Philosophy* 18, no. 4 (1988): 812–13. In his review of Nussbaum's *The Fragility of Goodness*, Taylor suggests that one does not have to opt for either the human standpoint – and not depart from there – or self-transcendence. 'The striving to surpass ourselves can also be seen as essentially human (on the inclusive interpretation). And what is more, the transcendent can be seen as endorsing or affirming the value of ordinary human attention and concern, as has undoubtedly been the case with the Judaeo-Christian tradition, with decisive consequences for our whole moral outlook.' See my article 'Mutilating Desire? Lonergan and Nussbaum: A Dialectic Encounter,' *Method: Journal of Lonergan Studies* 17 (Spring 1999): 1–26.

99 Taylor, *Sources of the Self*, 43.

100 Ibid., 47.

101 Ibid. 'In order to have a sense of who we are, we have to have a notion of how we become, and of where we are going ... that from a sense of what we have become, among a range of present possibilities, we project our future being.'

102 Ibid.

103 Ibid., 92.

104 Ibid., 47.

105 Ibid., 105.
106 Ibid., 92–3. Also see Taylor, 'The Diversity of Goods,' in *Philosophy and the Human Sciences.*
107 Ibid.
108 Ibid.
109 Ibid. In his 'Cross-Purposes: The Liberal-Communitarian Debate' (in *Philosophical Arguments*, 181–203), Taylor distinguishes between 'mediately' common goods, and 'immediately' common good. An example of a mediately common good would be a sharing between two people their love for Bach. 'But there are other things we value even more, like friendship itself, where what centrally matters to us is just that there are common actions and meanings. The good is that we share. This I call an 'immediately' common good.' *Philosophical Arguments*, 190.
110 Taylor, *Sources of the Self*, 63.
111 Ibid.
112 Ibid., 65.
113 Ibid., 66.
114 Ibid., 71.
115 Ibid., 85.
116 Ibid., 100.
117 Taylor, *Human Agency and Language*, 36.
118 Taylor, *Sources of the Self*, 80.
119 Ibid., 526. 'Transcending the self in terms of the model I'm [Taylor] working with here is to escape identification with a particular voice in the conversation, no longer to be the one who stands in a certain perspective in moral space.'
120 Taylor, *Human Agency and Language*, 16.
121 Ibid., 17.
122 Ibid., 18–19.
123 Taylor, *Sources of the Self*, 20.
124 Taylor, *Human Agency and Language*, 25.
125 Ibid.
126 Ibid., 31.
127 Ibid., 36.
128 Ibid.
129 Charles Taylor, 'Reply and Re-articulation,' *Philosophy in an Age of Pluralism* (Cambridge: Cambridge University Press, 1994), 219.
130 Taylor, *Philosophical Arguments*, 11.
131 Ibid.
132 Ibid., 42. See also Taylor, 'Reply and Re-articulation,' 220.
133 Taylor, *Sources of the Self*, 507.
134 Ibid., 419.
135 Ibid., 478.

136 Ibid., 428.

137 Taylor, *Ethics of Authenticity*, 87–9.

138 Taylor, *Sources of the Self*, 511.

139 Ibid., 425.

140 Ibid., 512.

141 Ibid., 510.

142 Charles Taylor, 'Heidegger, Language, and Ecology,' in *Heidegger: A Critical Reader*, ed. Hubert L. Dreyfus and Harrison Hall (Oxford: Blackwell, 1993), 247. In this essay, Taylor sees nature or the world as something that makes demands upon us, or calls us.

143 Taylor, *Sources of the Self*, 512.

144 Ibid., 513.

145 Taylor, 'Reply and Re-articulation,' 242.

146 Taylor, *Sources of the Self*, 481.

147 Ibid., 482.

148 Eric Voegelin, *In Search of Order*, vol. 5 of *Order and History* (Baton Rouge: Louisiana State University Press, 1987). It seems to me that there is something similar to what Voegelin is trying to articulate here in vol. 5 and Taylor's project. With respect to the nature of order, Voegelin speaks of a quest. 'For the story of the quest can be a true story only if the questioner participates existentially in the comprehending story told by the It through its creative epiphany structure' (27). Further on in this chapter Voegelin speaks about a 'beyond.' 'The question must be raised, because the "beyond" in the preceding sentence obviously is not a spatial preposition ... but rather a symbol expressing the participation of the temporal story in the dimension of the It-reality out-of- time. The presence of the divine Beyond of the formative Nous is experienced as the formative force in the philosopher's quest for truth' (30). And lastly, 'The Beyond is understood not to be a thing among things, but is experienced only in its formative presence, in its Parousia' (31).

149 Rainer Maria Rilke, 'The Ninth Elegy,' in *The Duino Elegies*, trans. Robert Hunter (Eugene, OR: Hulogosi Press, 1989), http://www.hunterarchive.com/files/Poetry/Elegies/elegy9.html.

150 Taylor, *Ethics of Authenticity*, 121.

Chapter 3: Bernard Lonergan: On Being Oneself

 1 John van Buren, *The Young Heidegger* (Bloomington: Indiana University Press, 1994), 134.

 2 Frederick Lawrence, 'The Hermeneutic Revolution and the Future of Theology,' in *Between the Human and the Divine*, ed. Andrzej Wiercinski (Toronto: Hermeneutic Press, 2002), 329.

 3 Ibid.

 4 Ibid., 329–30.

5 Bernard Lonergan, *Method in Theology* (London: Darton, Longman and Todd, 1971), 104.
6 Ibid., 243.
7 Bernard Lonergan, *Collection* (Montreal: Palm, 1967), 241. Lonergan is concerned in somewhat the way Adorno is with respect to language becoming too removed from the concrete flow of human existence. 'Of the human substance it is true that human nature is always the same; a man is a man whether he is awake or asleep, young or old, sane or crazy, sober or drunk, a genius or a moron, a saint or a sinner. From the viewpoint of substance, those differences are merely accidental. But they are not accidental to the subject, for the subject is not an abstraction; he is a concrete reality, all of him.'
8 Bernard Lonergan, *Insight*, vol. 3 of *Collected Works of Bernard Lonergan*, ed. Frederick E. Crowe and Robert M. Doran (Toronto: University of Toronto Press, 1992), 210.
9 Ibid.
10 Nicholas Plants, 'Lonergan and Taylor,' *Method: Journal of Lonergan Studies* 19, no. 1 (2001): 148. See also Charles Taylor, 'What Is Human Agency?' in *Human Agency and Language*, 15–44 (Cambridge: Cambridge University Press, 1985). Taylor introduces the notion of the affirmation of ordinary life to show how the whole of one's life can be a call to holiness.
11 Lonergan, *Collection*, 240.
12 Ibid.
13 Bernard Lonergan, *Phenomenology and Logic*, vol. 18 of *Collected Works of Bernard Lonergan*, ed. Philip J. McShane (Toronto: University of Toronto Press, 2001), 315.
14 Robert N. Bellah, William M. Sullivan, Ann Swidler, and Steven M. Tipton, *Habits of the Heart* (San Francisco: Harper and Row, 1985), 150. For example, Bellah points out the conflicting sets of ideals that seem to inform the hearts of Americans: 'Rather we found all the classic polarities of American individualism still operating: the deep desire for autonomy and self-reliance combined with an equally deep conviction that life has no meaning unless shared with others in the context of community.'
15 Bernard Lonergan, *A Third Collection*, ed. Frederick E. Crowe (New York: Paulist, 1985), 234.
16 Bernard Lonergan, *A Second Collection* (Philadelphia: Westminster, 1974), 69.
17 Ibid., 162.
18 Lonergan, *Insight*, 210–11.
19 Leon Kass, *The Hungry Soul* (New York: Free Press, 1994), 154.
20 Lonergan, *Insight*, 210–11.
21 Ibid.
22 Ibid., 215–27. Dramatic bias is not the only bias that concerns Lonergan. There is the problem of group bias, and probably the most pernicious form of bias –

general bias. Briefly, general bias eschews theory for the sake of practicality. Common-sense knowing sees itself as omni-competent. Common sense is concerned with the concrete and particular. It is an important mode of knowing. However, the problem with common sense is it 'easily is led to rationalize its limitations by engendering a conviction that other forms of human knowledge are useless or doubtfully valid.' Ibid., 251. See chapter 6 and 7 in *Insight* for a fuller account of bias and common-sense knowing and the relation between the two.

23 Ibid.
24 Ibid.
25 Ibid.
26 Ibid.
27 Ibid.
28 Ibid.
29 Ibid.
30 Lonergan, *Phenomenology and Logic*, 292.
31 Bernard Lonergan, *Understanding and Being*, vol. 5 of *Collected Works of Bernard Lonergan*, ed. Elizabeth A. Morelli and Mark D. Morelli (Toronto: University of Toronto Press, 1990), 182.
32 Lonergan, *Phenomenology and Logic*, 315.
33 Ibid.
34 Bernard Lonergan, *Topics in Education*, vol. 10 of *Collected Works of Bernard Lonergan*, ed. Frederick E. Crowe and Robert M. Doran (Toronto: University of Toronto Press, 1993), 88–91.
35 Ibid., 90.
36 Lonergan, *Phenomenology and Logic*, 281–4.
37 Charles Taylor, *Sources of the Self* (Cambridge, MA: Harvard University Press, 1989), 448.
38 Lonergan, *Phenomenology and Logic*, 281–4.
39 Ibid., 289–90.
40 Ibid., 291–7.
41 Lonergan, *Understanding and Being*, 184.
42 A basic horizon is a fundamental and all-embracing realm of intellectual, moral, and religious involvement. In this realm, one is 'living in truth or falsity, value or disvalue, God or not God.' Bernard Tyrell, *Bernard Lonergan's Philosophy of God* (London: Gill and Macmillan, 1974), 53.
43 Tyrell, *Philosophy of God*, 32.
44 Lonergan, *Phenomenology and Logic*, 309.
45 Ibid.
46 Ibid., 303.
47 Ibid., 238.
48 Ibid., 230.
49 Lonergan, *Collection*, 241.

50 Lawrence, 'Hermeneutic Revolution,' 333.

51 Lonergan, *Collection*, 241.

52 Lonergan, *Second Collection*, 79ff.

53 Lonergan, *Collection*, 242. It is not to be implied that there are degrees of humanness. We are all human beings from conception to death. What Lonergan is getting at is the real issue of development. We not only develop biologically, chemically, physically, and psychically, but also intellectually, morally, and spiritually. We are all human beings, but we can surrender our capacity for personhood by being unreflective, unintelligent, inattentive, and irresponsible.

54 Lonergan, *Phenomenology and Logic*, 305.

55 Ibid., 225.

56 Fred Dallmayr, *Critical Encounters between Philosophy and Politics* (Notre Dame, IN: University of Notre Dame Press, 1987), 5.

57 Lonergan, *Understanding and Being*, 99.

58 Eric Voegelin, 'Gospel and Culture,' in *Published Essays, 1966–1985*, vol. 12 of *Collected Works* (Baton Rouge: Louisiana State University Press, 1990), 172–211.

59 Lonergan, *Method in Theology*, 38.

60 Lonergan, *Understanding and Being*, 229.

61 Lonergan, *Collection*, 238.

62 Lonergan, *Phenomenology and Logic*, 238.

63 Albert Borgmann, *Crossing the Postmodern Divide* (Chicago: University of Chicago Press, 1992), 10.

64 Lonergan, *Phenomenology and Logic*, 237.

65 Lonergan, *Collection*, 242.

66 Lonergan, *Phenomenology and Logic*, 239.

67 Lonergan, *Second Collection*, 84.

68 Lonergan, *Method in Theology*, 80. See also *Third Collection*, 120–3.

69 Lonergan, *Topics in Education*, 55.

70 Dallmayr, *Critical Encounters*, 59.

71 Lonergan, *Second Collection*, 152.

72 Lonergan, *Topics in Education*, 80.

73 Ibid.

74 Lonergan, *Second Collection*, 128.

75 What follows is clearly an abbreviated account of what Lonergan understands by intellectual, moral, and religious conversion. I would direct the reader to *Insight* and *Method in Theology* for a richer and more detailed account of this threefold notion of conversion.

76 Charles Taylor, *Philosophical Arguments* (Cambridge, MA: Harvard University Press, 1995), vii.

77 Ibid.

78 Ibid., vii–viii.

79 Ibid.

80 Michael McCarthy, 'Pluralism, Invariance, and Conflict (Bernard Lonergan on Invariants of Intentional Subjectivity),' *Review of Metaphysics* 51, no. 1 (Sept. 1997): 1–21.

81 Jerome Miller, 'A Reply to Michael Maxwell,' *Method: Journal of Lonergan Studies* 12, no. 1 (1994): 118.

82 Lonergan, *Insight*, 279. 'There are two types of knowing. Each is modified by its own development. They are opposed, for one arises through intelligent and reasonable questions and answers, and the other does not. They are linked together in man, who at once is an animal, intelligent, and reasonable. Unless they are distinguished sharply by a critical theory of knowledge, they become confused, to generate aberrations.'

83 Plants, 'Lonergan and Taylor,' 145. See also Michael McCarthy, *The Crisis of Philosophy* (Albany, NY: SUNY Press, 1990).

84 Lawrence, 'The Hermeneutic Revolution,' 347.

85 Frederick Lawrence, 'Lonergan: The Integral Post-Modern?' *Method: Journal of Lonergan Studies* 18, no. 2 (2000): 112.

86 Lonergan, *Collection*, 223.

87 Lonergan, *Insight*, 343.

88 Frederick Lawrence, 'The Fragility of Consciousness,' *Theological Studies* 54 (1993): 72–3.

89 Richard M. Liddy, *Transforming Light* (Collegeville, MN: Liturgical, 1993), 171.

90 Charles Taylor, *Human Agency and Language* (Cambridge: Cambridge University Press, 1985), 248.

91 Lonergan, *Method in Theology*, 77.

92 Ibid., 181. See also Giovanni B. Sala, *Lonergan and Kant*, trans. Joseph Spoerl, ed. Robert M. Doran (Toronto: University of Toronto Press, 1994), 30. Sala also makes it clear that intellectual conversion is most difficult because of the constant presence of the fact that we are also animals, biologically oriented to the world around us. This biological orientation manifests itself in what Lonergan calls 'the-already-out-there-now-real.' This already-out-there-now-real continues to perpetuate the myth that human knowing is in reality animal knowing. Lonergan explains the phrase 'already-out-there-now-real' in the following way. 'It is *already*: it is given prior to any questions about it. It is *out*: for it is the object of extroverted consciousness. It is *there*: as sense organs, so too sensed objects are spatial. It is *now*: for the time of sensing runs along with the time of what is sensed. It is *real*: for it is bound up with one's living and acting and so must be just as real as they are.' *Method in Theology*, 263.

93 Ibid., 175.

94 Ibid., 176.

95 Ibid., 13.

96 Lonergan, *Second Collection*, 128–9. 'Indeed, in my opinion, intellectual conversion is essentially simple. It occurs spontaneously when one reaches the age of

reason, implicitly drops earlier criteria of reality (are you awake? do you see it? is it heavy? etc.), and proceeds to operate on the criteria of sufficient evidence or sufficient reason.' Bernard Lonergan, *Doctrinal Pluralism* (Milwaukee: Marquette University Press, 1971), 36.

97 Lonergan, *Collection*, 206.

98 Taylor, *Philosophical Arguments*, 77.

99 Lonergan, *Insight*, 501.

100 Michael Rende, *Lonergan on Conversion* (Lanham, MD: University Press of America, 1991), 71.

101 Lonergan, *Second Collection*, 75.

102 Lawrence, 'Fragility of Consciousness,' 81. The virtually unconditioned is something that just happens to have its conditions fulfilled. There is nothing necessary about the fact that it is. It is the 'reflective act of understanding that grasps that the conditions for a prospective judgment are or are not fulfilled. If they are fulfilled, the prospective judgment is 'virtually' or [better I think] 'contingently' unconditioned.' Robert M. Doran, 'Intelligentia Fidei in *De Deo Trino: Pars Systematica*,' *Method: Journal of Lonergan Studies* 19, no. 1 (2001): 42.

103 Lonergan, *Understanding and Being*, 190.

104 Lonergan, *Insight*, 581.

105 Lonergan, *Third Collection*, 173. Lonergan, *Method in Theology*, 240: 'Moral conversion changes the criterion of one's decisions and choices from satisfaction to values ... As our knowledge of human reality increases, as our responses to human values are strengthened and refined, our mentors more and more leave us to ourselves so that our freedom may exercise its ever advancing thrust toward authenticity. So we move to the existential moment when we discover for ourselves that our choosing affects ourselves no less than the chosen or rejected objects, and that it is up to each of us to decide for himself what he is to make of himself.'

106 Lonergan, *Third Collection*, 157ff.

107 Lawrence, 'Fragility of Consciousness,' 72.

108 Lonergan, *Second Collection*, 81–2.

109 Lonergan, *Method in Theology*, 31.

110 Taylor, *Human Agency and Language*, 60.

111 Ibid., 61.

112 Ibid., 49.

113 Ibid., 30–1.

114 Ibid., 31.

115 Lonergan, *Second Collection*, 168.

116 Lonergan, *Method in Theology*, 50.

117 Ibid., 51. In *Insight*, Lonergan speaks of a triple cross-division of values. 'They are true insofar as the possible choice is rational, but false insofar as the possibility of the choice results from a flight from self-consciousness, or from rationalization, or from moral renunciation. They are terminal inasmuch as they

are objects for possible choices, but they are originating inasmuch as directly and explicitly or indirectly and implicitly the fact that they are chosen modifies our habitual willingness, our effective orientation in the universe, and so our contribution to the dialectical process of progress and decline. Finally, they are actual, or in process, or in prospect, according as they have been realized already, or are in course of being realized, or merely are under consideration' (624).

118 Lonergan, *Method in Theology*, 36.

119 Ibid., 37.

120 Patrick H. Byrne, 'Analogical Knowledge of God and the Value of Moral Endeavor,' *Method: Journal of Lonergan Studies* 11, no. 2 (1993): 116.

121 Lonergan, *Method in Theology*, 37.

122 Byrne, 'Analogical Knowledge,' 117. For Taylor, one's identity is defined by one's fundamental evaluations, that is by one's strong evaluations that are ultimately about the richness of one's life and the kind of persons we are now, and aspire to be in the future. *Sources of the Self*, 105.

123 Byrne, 'Analogical Knowledge,' 110.

124 Ibid., 116.

125 Lonergan, *Method in Theology*, 104. See also Walter LaCentra, *The Authentic Self: Toward a Philosophy of Personality* (New York: Peter Lang, 1987), 90: 'The ideal of moral authenticity one dedicates himself to is embodied in a hierarchical scale of values ranging from the lowest level of vital health values, through social and cultural values to personal and religious values. Thus, the morally converted person is someone who is attempting to adjust his priorities to accommodate the demands of an ever higher integration of value.'

126 Lonergan, *Method in Theology*, 105. Lonergan goes through an Augustinian reversal. Initially, knowing something was followed by loving it. Now, however, Lonergan sees, as did Pascal, that being in love is first and it is the knowing of what one loves that follows.

127 Rosemary Haughton, *The Passionate God* (New York: Paulist, 1981), 47.

128 Lonergan, *Third Collection*, 175.

129 Lonergan, *Method in Theology*, 122.

130 Bartholomew M. Kiely, *Psychology and Moral Theology* (Rome: Gregorian University Press, 1980), 28. (In fleshing out his notion of religious conversion Lonergan consistently uses the word *God*. To avoid any confusion I will simply adhere to Lonergan's usage.)

131 Lonergan, *Method in Theology*, 105. Questions about good and evil, progress and decline, what is worthwhile or not, are all in the last analysis questions about God. Is the universal ultimately intelligible? Is man the first and only instance of a moral being? Are all our aspirations to goodness to end in an abyss of nothingness? In short, the person's 'transcendental subjectivity is mutilated or abolished, unless he is stretching forth towards the intelligible, the unconditioned, the good of value' (103).

132 Ibid., 106.
133 Ibid., 109.
134 Ibid., 106.
135 There is an ongoing debate as to whether being in love with God is a fifth level of consciousness. I would point the reader to Michael Vertin's article 'Lonergan on Consciousness: Is There a Fifth Level?' *Method: Journal of Lonergan Studies* 12, no. 1 (1994): 1–36.
136 Ibid., 106.
137 Lawrence, 'Fragility of Consciousness,' 91.
138 Lonergan, *Method in Theology*, 116.
139 Ibid., 106.
140 Lonergan, *Insight*, 721.
141 Lonergan, *Third Collection*, 248.
142 Lonergan, *Insight*, 651.
143 Ibid., 712.
144 Ibid., 651.
145 Ibid., 655.
146 Martha C. Nussbaum, *Love's Knowledge* (New York: Oxford University Press, 1990), 380. For a fuller account, see my article 'Mutilating Desire? Lonergan and Nussbaum: A Dialectic Encounter,' *Method: Journal of Lonergan Studies* 17, no. 2 (1999): 1–26.
147 Nussbaum, *Love's Knowledge*.
148 Ibid.
149 Taylor, *Sources of the Self*, 519.
150 Ibid.
151 Ibid., 520.
152 Ibid., 521.
153 Lonergan, *Collection*, 206. Here Lonergan quotes approvingly from Emerich Coreth's *Metaphysik: Eine methodisch-systematische Grundlegung*: 'From this it follows that there never is and never can be a closed 'inner area' of transcendental subjectivity, for subjectivity in its very performance is already 'outside' in the realm of being-in-itself in general which transcends subjectivity.'
154 Lonergan, *Method in Theology*, 116.
155 Ibid., 117.
156 Julian of Norwich, *All Shall Be Well* (Harrisburg, PA: Morehouse, 1992), 86.
157 Lonergan, *Third Collection*, 132.
158 Ibid., 133.

Chapter 4: Taylor and Lonergan: Dialogue and Dialectic

1 Mark C. Taylor, *Journeys to Selfhood* (New York: Fordham University Press, 2000), 6.

2 Ernst Becker, in *The Birth and Death of Meaning* (New York: Free Press, 1971), argues that all cultures determine what it means to be a normal – in terms of our discussion an authentic – human being. The benefits of society are distributed in accordance with that vision. See also *Character and Social Structure* by Hans Gerth and C. Wright Mills (New York: Harcourt, Brace and World, 1953).

3 Frederick Lawrence, 'Lonergan: The Integral Post-Modern?' *Method: Journal of Lonergan Studies* 18, no. 2 (2000): 115.

4 Both Taylor and Lonergan take seriously the displacement of the subject as the primary object of the universe. However, they also, contrary to certain forms of postmodernism, take seriously certain exigencies of human nature. See Maeve Cook's review of Ferrara's *Reflective Authenticity*, where she claims that Taylor's account of authentic subjectivity has its 'roots in a contentious philosophy of nature.' *Constellations* 5, no. 4 (1998): 573.

5 Taylor and Lonergan in their own way make clear that our subjectivity is a primordial nexus of relationships, and it is within this nexus where genuine human autonomy is grounded. In Trilling's *Sincerity and Authenticity* unfettered autonomy is really schizophrenia (suggested by a conversation with Michael McCarthy at the June 2006 Lonergan workshop at Boston College).

6 Lawrence, 'Lonergan: The Integral Post-Modern?' 120.

7 Lawrence, 'The Hermeneutic Revolution and the Future of Theology,' in *Between the Human and the Divine*, ed. Andrzej Wiercinski (Toronto: Hermeneutic Press, 2002), 346.

8 Ibid., 349.

9 Charles Taylor, *Sources of the Self* (Cambridge, MA: Harvard University Press, 1989), 18.

10 Ibid., 507.

11 Ibid., 456.

12 Ibid., 482.

13 Ibid., 454.

14 Ibid.

15 Ibid., 476.

16 Ibid., 491.

17 Ibid.

18 For example, Taylor points to Rilke's image of the angel. There may be some general belief around this particular image, but as Taylor makes clear, Rilke is articulating a vision of angelic being that is radically outside of any traditional understanding.

19 Taylor, *Sources of the Self*, 492.

20 Cited in ibid., 493.

21 Ibid., 491–2.

22 Ibid.

23 Bernard Lonergan, *Topics in Education*, vol. 10 of *Collected Works of Bernard Loner-*

gan, ed. Frederick E. Crowe and Robert M. Doran (Toronto: University of Toronto Press, 1993), 214.

24 Robert Brustein, 'Culture by Coercion,' *New York Times*, 29 Nov. 1994. Brustein maintains that art today is being instrumentalized to fit various political and social agendas. He quotes de Tocqueville to contextualize his argument: 'Democratic nations will habitually prefer the useful to the beautiful, and they will require that the beautiful be useful.'

25 Bernard Lonergan, *Insight*, vol. 3 of *Collected Works of Bernard Lonergan*, ed. Frederick E. Crowe and Robert M. Doran (Toronto: University of Toronto Press, 1992), 208.

26 Ibid.

27 Lonergan, *Topics in Education*, 211.

28 Ibid.

29 Bernard Lonergan, *Method in Theology* (London: Darton, Longman and Todd, 1971), 62.

30 Lonergan, *Topics in Education*, 222.

31 Lonergan, *Insight*, 209.

32 Ibid.

33 Bernard Lonergan, *A Third Collection*, ed. Fred Crowe (New York: Paulist, 1985), 28–9.

34 Ibid., 29. Sublation is dealt with later on in this chapter. For now let me quote from Lonergan on 'an intentionality analysis that distinguishes four levels of conscious and intentional operations, where each successive level sublates previous levels by going beyond them, by setting up a higher principle, by introducing new operations, and by preserving the integrity of previous levels, while extending enormously their range and their significance.' *Method in Theology*, 340.

35 Frederick Lawrence, 'The Ethics of Authenticity and the Human Good,' 6–7.

36 Frederick Lawrence, 'The Fragility of Consciousness,' *Theological Studies* 54 (1993): 182.

37 Charles Taylor, *Philosophical Arguments* (Cambridge, MA: Harvard University Press, 1995), 11.

38 Ibid., 23.

39 Lawrence, 'Fragility of Consciousness,' 59.

40 Giovanni B. Sala, *Lonergan and Kant*, trans. Joseph Spoerl, ed. Robert Doran (Toronto: University of Toronto Press, 1994), 75.

41 Taylor, *Philosophical Arguments*, 15.

42 Frederick Lawrence, 'Gadamer and Lonergan,' *International Philosophical Quarterly* 20, no. 1 (March 1980), 37.

43 Frederick Lawrence, 'The Ethics of Authenticity and the Human Good,' unpublished paper, 6–7.

44 Ibid., 14. It bears repeating: the use of the term *total* means the full hermeneutic exploration of the intentional subject as cognitional and completely concrete. It

is not a totalizing that privileges one position at the expense of the full range of concerns of the existential subject.

45 Taylor, *Philosophical Arguments*, 4.
46 Joseph Flanagan, *Quest for Self-Knowledge* (Toronto: University of Toronto Press, 1997), 268.
47 Lawrence, 'Fragility of Consciousness,' 187.
48 Ibid.
49 Michael McCarthy, 'Pluralism, Invariance and Conflict,' *Review of Metaphysics* 51, no. 1 (Sept. 1997): 9.
50 Lawrence, 'Fragility of Consciousness,' 198.
51 Ibid., 199.
52 Lonergan, *Third Collection*, 18.
53 Bernard Lonergan, *Second Collection* (Philadelphia: Westminster, 1974), 87.
54 Lonergan, *Method*, 41.
55 Ibid., 43.
56 Taylor, *Philosophical Arguments*, 5.
57 Taylor, *Sources of the Self*, 50.
58 Lonergan, *Insight*, 735.
59 Ibid., 738.
60 Taylor, *Philosophical Arguments*, 53.
61 Taylor, *Sources of the Self*, 448.
62 Ibid., 112.
63 Ibid.
64 Flanagan, *Quest for Self-Knowledge*, 252.
65 Lonergan, *Method in Theology*, 116.
66 Charles Taylor, *A Catholic Modernity?* (Oxford: University of Oxford Press, 1999), 21.
67 Ibid.
68 Ibid., 35.
69 Ibid., 26–7.
70 Lonergan, *Method in Theology*, 117.
71 Ibid., 118.
72 Charles Taylor, *Varieties of Religion Today* (Cambridge, MA: Harvard University Press, 2002), 115–16.
73 Charles Taylor, *The Ethics of Authenticity* (Cambridge, MA: Harvard University Press, 1992), 91.
74 Ibid., 40.
75 Charles Taylor, *Human Agency and Language* (Cambridge: Cambridge University Press, 1985), 95.
76 Charles Taylor, *Philosophy and the Human Sciences* (Cambridge: Cambridge University Press, 1985), 236.
77 Ibid., 238.

78 The taint would result from what we laid out earlier on Lonergan: the problem of bias, individual, group, and general.

79 Nicholas Plants, 'Lonergan and Taylor,' *Method: Journal of Lonergan Studies* 19, no. 1 (2001): 157.

80 Taylor, *Philosophical Arguments*, vii.

81 Ibid., 82.

82 Taylor, *Philosophy and the Human Sciences*, 182.

83 Taylor, *Human Agency*, 31.

84 Ibid., 26. It is important to remember, however, that Taylor is interested in a normative human nature, but not in terms of the old metaphysical 'essentialism.'

85 It might be best to be very clear about the use of the term *object*. As used throughout this work, an object is anything one can ask questions about. Meanings are objects, God is an object, trees are objects, and so forth.

86 Lonergan, *Third Collection*, 104.

87 Taylor, *Philosophy and the Human Sciences*, 11.

88 Lawrence, 'Gadamer and Lonergan,' 40.

89 Charles Taylor, 'Reply and Re-articulation,' in *Philosophy in an Age of Pluralism: The Philosophy of Charles Taylor in Question* (Cambridge: Cambridge University Press, 1994), 221.

90 Lonergan, *Method in Theology*, 89.

91 Ibid., 67.

92 Taylor, 'Reply and Re-articulation,' 221.

93 Flanagan, *Quest for Self-Knowledge*, 119.

94 Sala, *Lonergan and Kant*, 115.

95 Taylor, *Ethics of Authenticity*, 32–3.

96 Taylor, *Philosophical Arguments*, 32.

97 Ibid., 33.

98 Lonergan, *Third Collection*, 19.

99 Ibid., 156.

100 James Fenton, 'Subversives,' *New York Review of Books* 43, no. 1 (11 Jan. 1996), 51.

101 Lawrence, 'The Fragility of Consciousness,' 195.

102 Ibid.

103 Lonergan, *Second Collection*, 70–1.

104 Lonergan, *Third Collection*, 143.

105 McCarthy, 'Pluralism, Invariance and Conflict,' 10.

106 'These precepts are normative because they are given in the dynamic operations of human consciousness. Attending to one's own intelligence brings to light a primitive and basic meaning of the word, *normative*, for the intelligence in each of us prompts us to seek understanding, to be dissatisfied with a mere glimmer, to keep probing for an ever fuller grasp ... Our reasonableness demands sufficient evidence ... Finally there is the normativeness of deliberations. Between necessity and impossibility lies the realm of freedom and responsibility.' *Third Collection*, 143.

107 Ibid.
108 Ibid.
109 Lawrence, 'The Fragility of Consciousness,' 72.
110 Lonergan, *Third Collection*, 29.
111 Lonergan, *Method in Theology*, 13.
112 Taylor, *Philosophical Arguments*, 23.
113 Taylor, *Sources of the Self*, 72.
114 Ibid.
115 Ibid.
116 Ibid.
117 Ibid.
118 Ibid.
119 Ibid., 75.
120 Ibid., 72.
121 Taylor's account of this experience is somewhat analogous to what we described earlier concerning Eric Voegelin's account of pulls (*helkein*) and counterpulls (*anthelkein*). The one invites to life and light, the other to darkness and death. See also Voegelin's *Plato and Aristotle*, vol. 3 of *Order and History* (Baton Rouge: Louisiana State University Press, 1957).
122 Taylor, *Sources of the Self*, 74.
123 Ibid.
124 Ibid., 75.
125 Ibid., 65.
126 Ibid., 69–70.
127 Ibid., 106–7.
128 Ibid., 519.
129 Lonergan, *Method in Theology*, 31.
130 Robert M. Doran, *Psychic Conversion and Theological Foundations* (Chico, CA: Scholars, 1981), 65.
131 Ibid.
132 Ibid.
133 Lonergan, *Method in Theology*, 32.
134 Ibid., 109, 39.
135 Doran, 71–2.
136 Ibid., 71.
137 Ibid.
138 Taylor, *Sources of the Self*, 72.
139 Doran, *Psychic Conversion*, 76.
140 Ibid.
141 Lonergan, *Method in Theology*, 241.
142 Ibid.
143 Ibid., 242.
144 Ibid., 122.

145 Lawrence, 'Fragility of Consciousness,' 210.
146 Lonergan, *Third Collection*, 131.
147 Ibid., 131.
148 Sala, *Lonergan and Kant*, 74.
149 Lawrence, 'Fragility of Consciousness,' 209.
150 Lonergan, *Method in Theology*, 115.
151 Ibid., 116.
152 Ibid.

Conclusion

 1 Charles Taylor, *Sources of the Self* (Cambridge, MA: Harvard University Press, 1989), 448.
 2 Ibid., 449.
 3 Ibid., 133.
 4 Ibid., 144.
 5 Ibid., 133–4.
 6 Ibid., 450.
 7 Bernard Lonergan, *Method in Theology* (London: Darton, Longman and Todd, 1971), 254.
 8 Ibid., 53.
 9 Ibid., 55.
10 Taylor, *Sources of the Self*, 451.
11 Ibid., 452. See Lonergan's *Topics in Education* for an account of how the human good dialectically unfolds in history.
12 Bernard Lonergan, *Third Collection*, ed. Fred Crowe (New York: Paulist, 1985), 10.
13 Ibid.
14 Taylor, *Sources of the Self*, 449.
15 Ibid., 451. Here Taylor is speaking of Dostoevsky. However, I take Taylor to be in agreement with these sentiments.
16 Louis Roy, *Transcendent Experiences: Phenomenology and Critique* (Toronto: University of Toronto Press, 2001), 196.
17 Lonergan, *Third Collection*, 158.

Bibliography

Abbey, Ruth, ed. *Charles Taylor*. Cambridge: Cambridge University Press, 2004.

Adorno, Theodor W. *The Jargon of Authenticity*. Evanston, IL: Northwestern University Press, 1973.

Baynes, Kenneth, James Bohman, and Thomas McCarthy, eds. *After Philosophy: End or Transformation?* Cambridge, MA: MIT Press, 1993.

Becker, Ernest. *The Birth and Death of Meaning*. New York: Free Press, 1971.

Bellah, Robert N., William M. Sullivan, Ann Swidler, and Steven M. Tipton. *Habits of the Heart: Individualism and Commitment in American Life*. San Francisco: Harper and Row, 1986.

Berkowitz, Peter. *Nietzsche: The Ethics of an Immoralist*. Cambridge, MA: Harvard University Press, 1995.

Borgmann, Albert. *Crossing the Postmodern Divide*. Chicago: University of Chicago Press, 1992.

Braman, Brian J. 'Mutilating Desire? Lonergan and Nussbaum: A Dialectic Encounter.' *Method: Journal of Lonergan Studies* 17, no. 1 (1999): 1–26.

Brustein, Robert. 'Culture by Coercion.' *New York Times*, 29 November 1994.

Byrne, Patrick H. 'Analogical Knowledge of God and the Value of Moral Endeavor.' *Method: Journal of Lonergan Studies* 11, no. 2 (1993): 103–35.

Cook, Maeve. Review of Alessandro Ferrara, *Modernity and Authenticity: A Study of the Social and Ethical Thought of Jean-Jacques Rousseau*. *Constellations* 5, no. 4 (1998): 572–5.

Dallmayr, Fred. *Critical Encounters between Philosophy and Politics*. Notre Dame, IN: University of Notre Dame Press, 1987.

Doran, Robert M. 'Intelligentia Fidei in *De Deo Trino, Pars Systematica*.' *Method: Journal of Lonergan Studies* 19, no. 1 (2001): 35–83.

– *Psychic Conversion and Theological Foundations: Toward a Reorientation of the Human Sciences*. Chico, CA: Scholar's Press, 1981.

Dreyfus, Hubert L., and Harrison Hall, eds. *Heidegger: A Critical Reader*. Oxford: Blackwell, 1993.

Fenton, James. 'Subversives.' *New York Review of Books* 48, no. 1 (11 January 1996): 51–4.

Ferrara, Alessandro. *Modernity and Authenticity: A Study of the Social and Ethical Thought of Jean-Jacques Rousseau*. Albany, NY: SUNY Press, 1993.

Flanagan, Joseph. *Quest for Self-Knowledge: An Essay in Lonergan's Philosophy*. Toronto: University of Toronto Press, 1997.

Gerth, Hans, and C. Wright Mills. *Character and Social Structure*. New York: Harcourt, Brace and World, 1953.

Guignon, Charles B., ed. *The Cambridge Companion to Heidegger*. Cambridge: Cambridge University Press, 1993.

– 'Heidegger's "Authenticity" Revisited.' *Review of Metaphysics* 38 (1984): 321–39.

– 'History and Commitment in the Early Heidegger.' In *Heidegger: A Critical Reader*, ed. Hubert L. Dreyfus and Harrison Hall. Oxford: Blackwell, 1992.

Haughton, Rosemary. *The Passionate God*. New York: Paulist, 1981.

Heidegger, Martin. *Being and Time*. Trans. John Macquarrie and Edward Robinson. New York: Harper and Row, 1962.

Kass, Leon. *The Hungry Soul: Eating and the Perfecting of Our Nature*. New York: Free Press, 1994.

Kerr, Fergus. 'Taylor's Moral Ontology.' In *Charles Taylor*, ed. Ruth Abbey, 84–104. Cambridge: Cambridge University Press, 2004.

Kiely, Bartholomew M. *Psychology and Moral Theology*. Rome: Gregorian University Press, 1980.

LaCentra, Walter. *The Authentic Self: Toward a Philosophy of Personality*. New York: Peter Lang, 1987.

Lasch, Christopher. *The Culture of Narcissism*. New York: Norton, 1991.

Lawrence, Frederick. 'The Ethics of Authenticity and the Human Good: Lonergan on Values.' Paper given at Boston College.

– 'The Fragility of Consciousness: Lonergan and the Postmodern Concern for the Other.' *Theological Studies* 54 (1993): 55–94.

– 'Gadamer and Lonergan: A Dialectical Comparison.' *International Philosophical Quarterly* 20, no. 1 (March 1980): 25–47.

– 'The Hermeneutic Revolution and the Future of Theology.' In *Between the Human and the Divine: Philosophical and Theological Hermeneutics*, ed. Andrzej Wiercinski. Toronto: Hermeneutic Press, 2002.

– 'Lonergan: The Integral Post-Modern?' *Method: Journal of Lonergan Studies* 18, no. 2 (2000): 95–122.

Liddy, Richard M. *Transforming Light: Intellectual Conversion in the Early Lonergan*. Collegeville, MN: Liturgical Press, 1993.

Lonergan, Bernard. *Collection*. Montreal: Palm, 1967.
– *Doctrinal Pluralism*. Milwaukee: Marquette University Press, 1971.
– *Insight: A Study of Human Understanding*. Ed. Frederick E. Crowe and Robert M. Doran. Vol. 3 of *Collected Works of Bernard Lonergan*. Toronto: University of Toronto Press, 1992.
– *Method in Theology*. London: Darton, Longman and Todd, 1971.
– *Phenomenology and Logic: The Boston College Lectures on Mathematical Logic and Existentialism*. Ed. Philip J. McShane. Vol. 18 of *Collected Works of Bernard Lonergan*. Toronto: University of Toronto Press, 2001.
– *A Second Collection*. Philadelphia: Westminster Press, 1974.
– *A Third Collection: Papers by Bernard Lonergan*. Ed. Frederick E. Crowe. New York: Paulist, 1985.
– *Topics in Education*. Ed. Frederick E. Crowe and Robert M. Doran. Vol. 10 of *Collected Works of Bernard Lonergan*. Toronto: University of Toronto Press, 1993.
– *Understanding and Being*. Ed. Elizabeth A. Morelli and Mark D. Morelli. Vol. 5 of *Collected Works of Bernard Lonergan*. Toronto: University of Toronto Press, 1990.
MacIntyre, Alasdair. *After Virtue*. Notre Dame, IN: University of Notre Dame Press, 1984.
Macomber, William B. *The Anatomy of Disillusion: Martin Heidegger's Notion of Truth*. Evanston, IL: Northwestern University Press, 1967.
McCarthy, Michael H. *The Crisis of Philosophy*. Albany, NY: SUNY Press, 1989.
– 'Pluralism, Invariance, and Conflict (Bernard Lonergan on Invariants of Intentional Subjectivity).' *Review of Metaphysics* 51, no. 1 (September 1997): 1–21.
Miller, Jerome. 'A Reply to Michael Maxwell.' *Method: Journal of Lonergan Studies* 12, no. 1 (1994): 109–19.
Nietzsche, Friedrich. *On the Advantage and Disadvantage of History for Life*. Indianapolis: Hackett, 1980.
Norwich, Julian of. *All Shall Be Well: Revelations of Divine Love*. Harrisburg, PA: Morehouse, 1992.
Nussbaum, Martha C. *Love's Knowledge: Essays on Philosophy and Literature*. New York: Oxford University Press, 1990.
Plants, Nicholas. 'Lonergan and Taylor: A Critical Integration.' *Method: Journal of Lonergan Studies* 19, no. 1 (2001): 143–72.
Rende, Michael. *Lonergan on Conversion: The Development of a Notion*. Lanham, MD: University Press of America, 1991.
Richardson, William J. *Heidegger: Through Phenomenology to Thought*. The Hague: Nijhoff, 1974.
– 'Heidegger's Fall.' *American Catholic Philosophical Quarterly* 69 (1995): 29–53.
Rilke, Rainer Maria. *The Duino Elegies*. Trans. Robert Hunter. Eugene, OR: Hulogosi Press, 1989. http://www.hunterarchive.com/files/Poetry/Elegies/Duino _Elegies .html.

Rossinow, Douglas. *The Politics of Authenticity: Liberalism, Christianity and the New Left in America*. New York: Columbia University Press, 1998.

Roy, Louis. *Transcendent Experiences: Phenomenology and Critique*. Toronto: University of Toronto Press, 2001.

Sala, Giovanni B. *Lonergan and Kant: Five Essays on Human Knowledge*. Trans. Joseph Spoerl. Ed. Robert M. Doran. Toronto: University of Toronto Press, 1994.

Sass, Louis A. *Madness and Modernism: Insanity in the Light of Modern Art, Literature, and Thought*. New York: Harper Collins, 1992.

Smith, Nicholas H. 'Taylor and the Hermeneutic Tradition.' In *Charles Taylor*, ed. Ruth Abbey, 29–53. Cambridge: Cambridge University Press, 2004.

Taylor, Charles. *A Catholic Modernity?* Oxford: Oxford University Press, 1999.

– 'Critical Notice.' *Canadian Journal of Philosophy* 18, no. 4 (1988): 805–14.

– *Cross-Purposes: The Liberal-Communitarian Debate*. Cambridge, MA: Harvard University Press, 1995.

– 'Engaged Agency and Background in Heidegger.' In *The Cambridge Companion to Heidegger*, ed. Charles Guignon, 202–21. Cambridge: Cambridge University Press, 1993.

– *The Ethics of Authenticity*. Cambridge, MA: Harvard University Press, 1991.

– 'Heidegger, Language, and Ecology.' In *Heidegger: A Critical Reader*, ed. Hubert L. Dreyfus and Harrison Hall, 247–69. Oxford: Blackwell, 1993.

– *Human Agency and Language: Philosophical Papers*, vol. 1. Cambridge: Cambridge University Press, 1985.

– *Multiculturalism and the Politics of Recognition*. Princeton, NJ: Princeton University Press, 1992.

– 'Overcoming Epistemology.' In *After Philosophy: End or Transformation?* ed. Kenneth Baynes, James Bohman, and Thomas McCarthy, 464–88. Cambridge, MA: MIT Press, 1993.

– *Philosophical Arguments*. Cambridge, MA: Harvard University Press, 1995.

– *Philosophy and the Human Sciences: Philosophical Papers*, vol. 2. Cambridge: Cambridge University Press, 1985.

– *Philosophy in an Age of Pluralism*. Cambridge: Cambridge University Press, 1994.

– 'Reply and Re-articulation.' In *Philosophy in an Age of Pluralism: The Philosophy of Charles Taylor in Question*, 213–57. Cambridge: Cambridge University Press, 1994.

– *Sources of the Self: The Making of the Modern Identity*. Cambridge, MA: Harvard University Press, 1989.

– *Varieties of Religion Today: William James Revisited*. Cambridge, MA: Harvard University Press, 2002.

Taylor, Mark C. *Journeys to Selfhood: Hegel & Kierkegaard*. New York: Fordham University Press, 2000.

Trilling, Lionel. *Sincerity and Authenticity*. Cambridge, MA: Harvard University Press, 1972.

Tully, James. 'Preface.' In *Philosophy in an Age of Pluralism: The Philosophy of Charles*

Taylor in Question, ed. James Tully, xiii–xvi. Cambridge: Cambridge University Press, 1994.

Tyrrell, Bernard. *Bernard Lonergan's Philosophy of God*. London: Gill and Macmillan, 1974.

van Buren, John. *The Young Heidegger: Rumor of the Hidden King*. Bloomington: Indiana University Press, 1994.

Vertin, Michael. 'Lonergan on Consciousness: Is There a Fifth Level?' *Method: Journal of Lonergan Studies* 12, no. 1 (1994): 1–36.

Voegelin, Eric. 'Gospel and Culture.' In *Published Essays, 1966–1985*. Vol. 12 of *Collected Works*. Baton Rouge: Louisiana State University Press, 1990.

– *Plato and Aristotle*. Vol. 3 of *Order and History*. Baton Rouge: Louisiana State University Press, 1957.

– *In Search of Order*. Vol. 5 of *Order and History*. Baton Rouge: Louisiana State University Press, 1987.

Wiercinski, Andrzej, ed. *Between the Human and the Divine: Philosophical and Theological Hermeneutics*. Toronto: Hermeneutic Press, 2002.

Zimmerman, Michael. *Eclipse of the Self: The Development of Heidegger's Concept of Authenticity*. Athens: Ohio University Press, 1986.

Index